MY
SOUL
IS
AMONG
LIONS

MY
SOUL
IS
AMONG
LIONS

PAGES FROM THE
BREAST CANCER ARCHIVES

ELLEN LEOPOLD
Valley Green Press

Copyright © 2013 by Ellen Leopold
Library of Congress Control Number: 2013957259
ISBN 978-0-9898737-0-3 (paperback)
ISBN 978-0-9898737-2-7 (e-book)

"Body Language" first appeared in *The Nation*,
December 1996.

"Obituaries: Baring the Breast Alice James
to Kathy Acker" appeared in *Sojourner: The
Women's Forum*, March 1998.

"Shopping for the Cure" appeared in *The
American Prospect*, September 25–October
9, 2000.

"Unsung Heroines: Unveiling History: Janet
Elizabeth Lane-Claypon," written with Warren
Winkelstein Jr., May–June 2004; "Irma
Natanson and the Legal Landmark *Natanson
v. Kline*," Fall 2004; and "Barbie meets Breast
Cancer," September 2005, all appeared in the
newsletter for Breast Cancer Action.

Katharine Lee Bates, "For Katharine Coman's
Family and Innermost Circle of Friends"
appeared in *Legacy: A Journal of Women
Writers* 23/1 (2006), reprinted with permission
of the Margaret Clapp Library, Wellesley
College, Wellesley College Archives.

"'My Soul Is Among Lions': Katharine Lee
Bates's Account of the Illness and Death
of Katharine Coman" appeared in *Legacy:
A Journal of Women Writers* 23/1 (2006).

My soul is among lions:
and I lie even among them
that are set on fire, even the sons of men,
whose teeth are spears and arrows,
and their tongue a sharp sword.

—Psalm 57, 4

Contents

Introduction   ix

1   "My Soul Is Among Lions": Katharine Lee   1
Bates's Account of Illness and Death of
Katharine Coman

2   "For Katharine Coman's Family and   49
Innermost Circle of Friends"

3   An Unsung Heroine: Janet Elizabeth   83
Lane-Claypon

4   Irma Natanson and the Legal   89
Landmark *Natanson v. Kline*

5   Barbie Meets Breast Cancer   97

6   Body Language   105

7   The Last Word: Obituaries   123

8   Shopping for the Cure   145

9   The Tyranny of Cheerfulness: "Pink   157
Ribbons, Inc."

10   The Breast Cancer Donor's Dilemma: 165
Time to Revolt?

Acknowledgments   175

Notes   177

Introduction

I first wrote about breast cancer over twenty years ago, in 1992, with my friend Jean Hardisty. We were, at the time, both members of the Women's Community Cancer Project (WCCP), a group that met monthly at the Women's Center in Cambridge, Massachusetts. Aware that the nascent breast cancer movement had not yet addressed the problems of poverty, Jean and I decided to write about the extra obstacles facing low-income women diagnosed with cancer. We wrote a long piece for what was then the leading feminist newspaper in New England, *Sojourner: The Women's Forum*. Called "Cancer and Poverty: Double Jeopardy for Women," our article documented the health disparities that were closely allied to disparities in income, health insurance, and education.

This was not, it turned out, a major concern to either the medical establishment or the mainstream media, narrowly preoccupied as it was with reporting alleged scientific breatkthroughs.[1] In fact, much of what inflamed the passions of women in the Cancer Project was on no one's agenda at the time. Despite the fact that the disease was now claiming more than 40,000 American lives every year, criticizing the status quo—in print—was still rare. The WCCP helped to change that, publishing a regular newsletter that captured some of that passion on the page. The photo below, taken at a demonstration on the Boston Common in the fall of 1992, neatly summarizes the issues that galvanized the group at the time, all of which were taken

up—many repeatedly—in articles published in the newsletter.

Over the next several years, WCCP members (including myself) contributed stories that seemed to challenge almost every aspect of the disease, questioning the lack of progress in stemming the rising tide of deaths, the limitations of mammography, the continued reliance on toxic and disfiguring treatments, and increasingly important, the apparent indifference to prevention, marked by the failure to investigate possible links between environmental poisons and cancer causation.

The lack of forward momentum piqued my curiosity. Why, I wanted to know, was the experience at the end of the twentieth century so depressingly similar to what it had been a half-century earlier? Where were the thousands of women who had suffered and died from the disease before us? What did they have to tell us? I was, essentially, looking for the backstory of breast cancer, or at least for some fragments of it that would shed light on the social, rather than the medical side of its history. What role did culture play in mediating the pace of change? And why did it take so long for women to understand the disease as a feminist issue?

I tried to provide some answers to these questions in *A Darker Ribbon: Breast Cancer, Women, and*

Their Doctors in the Twentieth Century (1999). Two correspondences lie at the heart of this book, each between a woman diagnosed with breast cancer and her surgeon, each running from diagnosis to death. The first set of letters, from 1917 to 1922, was exchanged between a doctor's daughter and William Stewart Halsted, the first professor of surgery at the Johns Hopkins Medical School; the second between Rachel Carson and Dr. George Crile Jr. at the Cleveland Clinic, from 1960 to 1964. Though separated by more than forty years, the two women faced similar ordeals. For both, the surgeon was still male, still the gatekeeper to breast cancer treatment, and still reluctant to disclose the truth to his patient. Both women's experience was dominated by the procedure for radical mastectomy, which Halsted himself had introduced at the end of the nineteenth century. This remained the "gold standard" of treatment for almost a century, when surgery was king. With no competing therapies beating at the door, Halsted's operation was never forced to prove its effectiveness despite a death rate that almost doubled over this period—from 7.8 breast cancer deaths in 1922 for every 100,000 people to 13.7 in 1964.

The book goes on to explore the efforts made by many women—and a few enlightened male doctors—to rouse the disease from its torpor and lift it out of its medical backwater. Along the way, I caught a glimpse of some intriguing figures who lay just beyond the scope of the story I was then telling. I was determined to go back for them when I could.

Many of the articles and essays gathered here are the fruits of these pursuits. Written between 1996 and 2012, all of them reach into corners of breast cancer history that until recently have attracted litt le attention. Some were written well before there was really an audience for them. Now there are over two million American women with a history of the disease and an appetite for knowing more than they can glean from the science pages of newspapers.

The book starts off with stories of individual women who were, in some way, agents of change. Taken together, they hint at the many kinds of damage an entrenched disease like breast cancer can inflict and the need to respond to it on many fronts. The women highlighted here—Katharine Lee Bates, memoirist; Janet Lane-Claypon, epidemiologist; Irma Natanson, plaintiff; and Ruth Handler, inventor; are just a very few of those who made a difference.

The longest of these pieces is a memoir by

Katharine Lee Bates, recounting the illness and death of her life companion, Katharine Coman, who died of breast cancer in 1915. My introduction to this memoir tries to make clear just how unusual—and revealing—a document it is.

The shorter pieces on Lane-Claypon, Natanson, and Handler that follow emphasize the difficulties facing those who would challenge the status quo. These women marshaled the resources they had at their disposal and put them to new uses. Lane-Claypon pioneered the emerging discipline of breast cancer epidemiology. Natanson, damaged by cobalt radiation treatment, took her grievances to court and, in the process, strengthened legal protections for women through the doctrine of informed consent. Handler, outraged by the lack of decent post-mastectomy prostheses, decided she could do better—and did.

Only Handler, the youngest of these four women (she died in 2002) ever wrote for publication about her personal experience of the disease. But until relatively recently, this was the prescribed path to publication for most books on the subject (excluding self-help guides written by doctors and nutritionists). The worlds of activist newsletters and mainstream publishing rarely overlapped. If breast cancer had a literature, it was confined to chronicles of the disease as a personal journey. Such books posed no threat to the medical establishment. They were, typically, confessional and well behaved; their authors were reluctant to consider their own struggles as symptomatic of problems afflicting *all* women with the disease. There were exceptions like Rose Kushner's *Breast Cancer: A Personal History and Investigative Report* (1975). But even she had to adopt the approved format and deliver her criticisms from inside a personal narrative. The review titled "Body Language" considers this tradition, its limitations and eventual disappearance—or, more accurately, transformation.

"The Last Word," the essay that follows it, also examines the representation of breast cancer on the printed page. In this case, it traces the tortured history of obituaries as they grapple with the increasing visibility of women and a disease that would not go away but could not be named.

Finally, the book pulls away from the personal, in line with recent shifts in media attention. Changes in corporate philanthropy have had a significant impact on the perception of breast cancer. Companies have now turned away from general giving toward charitable causes that enhance their bottom line. "Pink ribbon" marketing is a by-product of this shift, as Samantha King documents in her book, reviewed in "The Tyranny of Cheerfulness." The rise to prominence of national breast cancer charities and their sponsorship by big business has made breast cancer a magnet for journalistic coverage that is altogether more "corporate" in outlook, concerned as much with issues of executive compensation and board membership as with evaluating their success in accomplishing the mission that gave them life to begin with.

The alliance between business and breast cancer has created a powerful new hybrid, one that does not seem to have accelerated progress towards either prevention or cure. I was troubled by this in 2000 ("Shopping for the Cure") and I remain troubled by this today ("The Breast Cancer Donor's Dilemma: Time to Revolt?").

ཀྱི་ཀྱི་ཀྱི་

Where conditions have materially changed over the intervening years, I have added commentary to update them. These latter-day adjustments give some idea of the pace of progress—or lack of it.

1 ❦
"My Soul Is Among Lions": Katharine Lee Bates's Account of the Illness and Death of Katharine Coman

By the end of the twentieth century, breast cancer narratives constituted a genre of their own. What had begun in the United States in the 1970s with a few scattered memoirs had, by the late 1990s, become a veritable torrent.[2] The popularity of these narratives marked the final—and irreversible—lifting of the veil from a disease that, with few exceptions, had been hidden away since time immemorial. The new genre also delineates significant changes in the course of the disease itself.

This article first appeared in *Legacy: A Journal of Women Writers* 23/1 (2006).

Earlier diagnosis and treatment now gave women many more years of life. Suddenly transformed into breast cancer "survivors," women were surprised to discover that they had lived to tell their tale and were eager— and extremely grateful—for the opportunity to do so. Fortified by second-wave feminism, they picked up their pens. Casting themselves as reluctant heroines, the writers trace their dangerous passage through a dark thicket of toxic treatments. Ultimately they prevail, regaining a place of relative safety in their former lives.[3]

The proliferation of these accounts has naturally crowded out the earlier and much deadlier experience of breast cancer among American women. Until the 1970s, there waslittle evidence that the disease actually existed. Although it killed more than a million American women in the first six decades of the twentieth century, breast cancer was never acknowledged in any public arena—not in the press, on television or radio, nor in any books written for a lay audience. Whatever evidence survives of the early twentieth-century experience of the disease, therefore, must come from private sources. But for families with a breast cancer history, there may have been little incentive to hold on to anything that kept their pain alive and fresh. Whether described in diaries or letters, the illnesses these families endured could last for several years and would be full of terrible disfigurement and pain. Unlike contemporary accounts, letters and diaries written before the 1970s record no return journeys to the land of the living; rather, there is an inexorable decline into suffering and death. Such accounts would not only be difficult to reread, but they might also be a source of family shame, to be destroyed as quickly as possible.

The scarcity of surviving evidence from the early twentieth century makes Katharine Lee Bates's 1915 unpublished narrative about the breast cancer and death of her partner of twenty-five years, Katharine Coman, all the more important.[4] During her lifetime, Katharine Lee Bates (1859–1929) was an academic and literary luminary.[5] Remembered today primarily as the woman who wrote the lyrics for "America the Beautiful," in her own time period Bates was an esteemed teacher, a prolific poet, and a widely published author.

Her partner, Katharine Coman (1857–1915), an economic historian and social reformer, was only slightly less well known.[6] Bates's narrative appears to be the earliest American account of breast cancer conceived explicitly as the history of an illness, written sixty years before the first published accounts began to appear.[7] Bates wrote the memorial in a concentrated burst of a few days, shortly after Coman's death, when the memory and pain of it were both still fresh. For the early twenty-first-century reader, Bates's narrative highlights the radical changes that have taken place over the past century in the way women experience and understand breast cancer. Her account also reveals the language, etiquette, and tropes of attachment between two educated women of the early twentieth century and the coterie of women who surrounded and supported them throughout their lives.

BREAST CANCER IN THE EARLY TWENTIETH CENTURY

By the time Katharine Coman was diagnosed with breast cancer, radical mastectomy had already become the standard treatment. The form of the procedure used in the United States was introduced by William Stewart Halsted (1852–1922) at Johns Hopkins. What he added to an operation that had been performed in one form or another since the Roman era was the routine removal of the breast together with the overlying skin, the underlying pectoral muscles, and the auxiliary lymph nodes, all taken in one piece (en bloc). This was almost certainly the version of the surgery that Coman underwent. It was, as its name implies, an extreme measure and one that carried considerable risks. "No one can deny," wrote the English cancer surgeon Geoffrey Keynes in 1937, "that radical surgery often entails, in addition to an appreciative operative mortality, a really hideous mutilation."[8]

Halsted was never able to prove the theory of disease that justified the radical removal of so much of a woman's upper body. But he did not have to. The absence of any competing therapy, combined with the rise of the new surgical profession, allowed him to position the procedure at the heart of breast cancer treatment, where it remained for almost a hundred years. Ultimately, Halsted was proven wrong; he had rejected the notion that cancer cells could travel out of the breast to other vital organs through the bloodstream—that breast cancer could quickly become a systemic disease rather than a localized one. Once metastasis was properly understood, it became clear that surgery on the breast was unlikely to be lifesaving, at least in the time period when breast lumps were typically discovered late in the course of the disease. No matter how much tissue and muscle were removed, by the time a woman submitted to surgery it was often too late.

In justifying his beliefs, Halsted relied on the work of a contemporary English surgeon, William

Sampson Handley (1872–1962), who also misunderstood the true nature of metastasis. Handley was as influential a promoter of the radical mastectomy in Britain as Halsted was in the United States. Handley was also the physician that Coman consulted in London when the symptoms of her own metastasized disease began to show themselves. These visits make it clear that Coman received what was, at the time, considered state-of-the-art advice and treatment.

As detailed in Bates's narrative, Coman first sought medical advice while she was living with her mother and sister in Chicago; she was operated on for the first time in the Newton (now Newton Wellesley) Hospital in June 1911. The exact nature of this surgery is unknown. In the fall of 1911, she discovered "a tiny lump" in her left breast but did not mention it to anyone, not even to Bates, until late spring 1912. She then immediately had a second, apparently more extensive procedure, almost exactly one year to the day after the first one, in the same hospital. The prognosis given afterward by one of the surgeons was grim: "The future will be short and troubled." In December 1913, she began to feel pain in her left side, which doctors diagnosed as rheumatism. In April, Handley also mistook her pains for rheumatism. However, two months later, upon learning of Coman's coughing and increasing breathlessness, he told Bates that "cancer was at work in the left lung and that Katharine could not live a year." Coman died seven months later, in January 1915.

In 1915, about 7,700 women died of breast cancer in the United States. Although the population of the country has tripled since then, the number of deaths from breast cancer has risen almost sixfold. This is one of the reasons that awareness of the disease has changed so radically since Coman's day. However, at the time Coman was diagnosed, the leading causes of death among Americans were still pneumonia and tuberculosis. Cancer was well down on the list. It remained obscure in every sense. And, of course, cancer of the breast suffered the additional stigma of association with a woman's body—a taboo against drawing public attention to it was firmly in place. Where the subject did surface in print, in medical texts or health manuals for women, the disease was often traced to "inappropriate" behavior on the part of the hapless female victim—too much dancing, exercising, or thinking were often cited as causes.[9]

The medical establishment showed little interest at the time in correcting the medieval superstitions and fatalism that dominated responses to the

7

disease or in looking for more scientifically sound explanations for its causes and behavior. There were a few exceptions. In 1915, the year of Coman's death, a statistician drew attention to the relatively higher death rates that prevailed among single women over the age of forty-five.[10] This was one of the first suggestions that environmental factors, broadly construed, might play a role in causing breast cancer and might even have played a role in Coman's own cancer history, although such an idea would never have occurred to either Coman or Bates. The first signs of public concern about the growing incidence of the disease began to appear about ten years after Coman's death. A government report published in 1925 documented an unprecedented increase in the number of breast cancer deaths between 1910 and 1920, a trend that would continue for the next seventy-five years.[11]

THE BATES-COMAN PARTNERSHIP

Bates and Coman were professors at Wellesley College in its early days as a college for women administered by women. Both were well-known figures in the group of talented women who taught at the college or formed its surrounding community. Bates's poems, stories, travel diaries, and essays appeared frequently in popular magazines,

from the *Churchman* and the Congregationalist,
where "America the Beautiful" first appeared, to
the *Atlantic Monthly* and *Life*. Bates also produced
commentaries on and scholarly editions of the
work of several writers, including Shakespeare and
Hawthorne. Interested in contemporary poetry all

KATHARINE LEE BATES

her life, she initiated a reading series at Wellesley that drew poets from around the world, including William Butler Yeats, Robert Frost, and Vachel Lindsay.

An able and patient administrator, Bates spent a great deal of her time shaping the new Department of English Literature at Wellesley. Her teaching methods were widely admired. Vida Dutton Scudder, an academic colleague, recalled that "she did not present her students with a problem to solve but with an experience to enter, which is a far more exacting and strenuous matter."[12]

Bates became a professor in 1891; Coman set up the Department of Economics and became a professor of economics and sociology in 1900. Coman, too, was prolific and talented. She wrote widely—and originally—in the new fields of economic and labor history. She was one of the first academics to undertake empirical research using overlooked materials, including government documents (congressional committee and statistical reports), state and local archives, and newspapers, thereby enriching her histories with a more vivid sense of lived experience. Her best-known book is probably *The Economic Beginnings of the Far West: How We Won the Land Beyond the Mississippi*.[13] Bates was instrumental in conceiving plans for

the first settlement house on the East Coast, but
it was Coman, the more politically engaged of the
two, who actually worked to set up the house in
Boston's South End in 1892. Both traveled exten-
sively, sometimes together, to California, Europe,
Scandinavia, and Egypt. They collaborated on a

KATHARINE COMAN

book called *English History Told by English Poets*, published in 1902.

The two women met at Wellesley and formed an attachment by 1890. Bates then left for a year's study in England. A letter she wrote to Coman from that period makes plain the intensity of her feelings: "It was never very possible to leave Wellesley [for good], because so many love-anchors held me there, and it seemed least of all possible when I had just found the long-desired way to your dearest heart. . . . Of course I want to come to you, very much as I want to come to Heaven" (24 February 1891).[14] Eventually, Bates and Coman built a house in the town of Wellesley and named it "The Scarab," commemorating a shared trip to Egypt. They lived there together in a loving relationship until Coman's death in January 1915.

"WORKING AS IN A DREAM"

What prompted Bates to undertake this posthumous account of her partner's ordeal? She does not say. Bates knew that Wellesley College would be putting together its own memorial to Coman that would showcase her impressive accomplishments.[15] This left her free to scale down her field of vision, to leave to others the litany of worldly achievements and concentrate instead on the details of their domestic life together. Bates's diary entries from the time show how much of an effort this might have been. In the weeks leading up to the first surgery, she confesses, "Still working as in a dream"; and ten days later, "In desperate need of distracting my thoughts from Katharine's ordeal now so close" (18 and 28 May 1911). The diary reports on hospital visits, on the details of Coman's post-operative recoveries (having her stitches and bandages removed), and on her state of mind: "so helpless but so brave and patient. I think my heart must be breaking" (6 June 1912). On 24 January 1915, mid-writing, she reflects, "I don't know why this heart of mine should go on beating when Katharine's heart is ashes—but it does." A few weeks later, having finished writing, she inscribes a line from a Walter Scott ballad— "My wound is deep; I fain would sleep" (24 January and 6 February 1915).

Yet none of these details nor the tone of distress they evoke are included in the illness narrative. Bates sees this document as serving a wider purpose, one that is separate from, if inevitably colored by her own grief. It is likely that she felt a sense of obligation to the close circle of women friends, colleagues, and relatives who had endured this terrible experience with her. For perhaps this reason, the memorial note was intended to be privately circulated. Bates clearly had a limited readership in mind: the two women's friends, relatives, and caregivers (paid as well as unpaid) are carefully—and artfully—included. As the title page explicitly states, the memoir was composed "For Katharine Coman's family and innermost circle of friends. Not for print nor in any way for general circulation." It was, as Bates put it, "only for the eyes of those who have love's right to see." A concern to protect the privacy of both women was at work here, possibly heightened by the delicacy of the subject. However, almost a century later, no one who knew either woman remains alive. More important in the decision to override her prohibition against publication, though, is that Bates left this memorial in the papers she bequeathed to Wellesley College, with no restrictions on its use.

THE INNERMOST CIRCLE OF FRIENDS

 The tight-knit circle Bates cites was an extraordinarily accomplished, if rarefied, group of women. Most of them had some association with Wellesley College, which, at a time when the further education of women was in its infancy, marked them as members of a tiny, privileged, white Protestant elite. Wellesley salaries were not overly generous, but they permitted these women to live independent lives and to retire with a guaranteed pension.[16] The group included Caroline Hazard (1856–1945), the president of Wellesley between 1899 and 1910, during which time she helped to double its enrollment and triple its endowment. Another friend was Eliza Mosher (1846–1928), one of the first women doctors trained in the United States, who later became the first woman dean and faculty member at the University of Michigan. Emily Balch (1867–1961), also a part of this illustrious group, became a widely respected social reformer, political activist, and peace advocate, winning the Nobel Peace Prize in 1946, only the second American woman to do so.[17]

Because none of the women married or had children, each lived what would have been thought of as an outlaw existence if she had lived alone. But the women's associations that began to emerge toward the end of the nineteenth century (women's colleges, settlement houses, etc.) provided models for alternative living arrangements that transformed professional colleagues into friends and intimates. The successful blending of public and private lives into comfortable communities was a demonstrable rebuff to the dire warnings that damned single intellectual women to lives of bitter loneliness.

For ambitious young women who chose not to marry, these ménages provided a feasible alternative to conventional domestic life. Scudder, a member of the Wellesley English Department who had been mentored by Bates and who had also bought a house near campus, describes the emergence of the new living arrangements in her memoir: "More and more, members of the college faculty were establishing homes in the town, as Katharine Bates and I had done; and we enjoyed, as we still do, interchange of ideas, friends, household problems, and seedlings. It was a good life."[18]

As a former student of Bates recalled, the joint household in Wellesley "was founded on the wonderful friendship of Miss Bates and Miss Katharine Coman. . . . It was as well the house of other friendships. One always knew welcome there, no matter how loudly the dogs might bark."[19] The domesticity here was dynamic, unlike that prevailing in more conventional middle-class homes. It could, without upheaval, accommodate the shifting composition of household members and long periods of absence as one or another of them visited far-flung relatives, traveled for purposes of research, or took sabbaticals.

This kind of open-ended family life served both

Coman and Bates well. In her last illness, Coman was not shut away in a darkened room in shame, as were many of her married contemporaries with the same disease. She was whisked off in carriages and "perambulators" to convalesce at the country homes of friends like Cornelia Warren and Emily Balch, where she was promised fresh air, fresh food, and a hammock in which to lie. Friends took over many "wifely" tasks to keep domestic spirits up, supplying everything from specially prepared buttermilk to a veritable greenhouse of fresh flowers. More important, Bates was spared the enforced secrecy and terror experienced by many husbands faced with the loss of a conjugal partner and housewife and the prospect of children soon to be bereaved. Bates also could anticipate the loving condolences, comfort, and practical support of other women when the end did come.

Arguably, it was the very strength of this sisterhood that both motivated Bates and empowered her to become the chronicler of her friend's suffering. Providing every kind of sympathetic care and support, their circle of friends spun a cushioned web of protection around both Bates and Coman. This cleared a space in the bleak days following Coman's death for Bates to try to make sense of it all for an audience sensitive to her situation. In effect, these women served as the equivalent, in Bates's time, of the much wider women's health networks in existence since the early 1990s that support women diagnosed with breast cancer (as well as other diseases), supplying them with information, encouragement, shared stories, and comfort food.

ACCOMMODATING THE DISEASE

No woman undergoing a radical mastectomy at the time Coman did would have known in advance just how extensive the surgery would be. Nor would she understand that, even if the prognosis were good, she would be permanently disabled and possibly in a state of unremitting pain. The chances of her knowing anyone who had undergone the same procedure were very slim indeed. The chances of her actually discussing such a procedure, even if she knew someone who was in a position to enlighten her, were even slimmer.[20] This ignorance was another clear expression of the absence of breast cancer from the culture. Women were not encouraged to be curious about their own bodies even when they were healthy. When they became seriously unhealthy, that lack of curiosity could become a violent aversion. Shame took over. Women who had to endure breast cancer surgery often hid their disease, even from members of their own families. It was not uncommon for children to be kept in the dark. The need to collude with the demand for secrecy must have added terrible distress to the physical pain women already faced.[21] Coman seems to have been spared this additional suffering. She gives no evidence of wanting to hide the gravity of her situation. Nor does Bates refrain from raising it among her friends.[22] Bates also knew other women with breast cancer.[23] Such openness must have been exceptionally rare.

Coman does, however, shy away from directly confronting either the physical details of her illness or its prognosis. "A physician consulted in Chicago," Bates writes early in the narrative, "had made the mistake, carried away by scientific enthusiasm, of showing her colored diagrams illustrating every phase of the critical surgery involved, and those pictures, with their suggestion of the desecration of the body, gave Katharine 'a nightmare week.'" A few years later in London, when Coman began to suffer "terrible paroxysms of coughing," she refused to countenance a return visit to the cancer specialist. Bates resorted to a subterfuge to leave the house in order to look up the specialist's address and write to him with an account of "recent developments." When his reply arrived at their breakfast table, Bates tried to hide it under the marmalade but Coman caught her at it and asked her to read the letter aloud. After listening to its dire report—"the symptoms were significant and alarming"—Coman, "without comment, took up the *Times* and gave me the morning news." There was to be no display of self-pity, no demonstrable panic at the prospect of mortality.

Coman's religious convictions played a central role in determining her response to illness. According to Scudder, "Close, devout intimacy with the Gospels was the basis of her teaching and her social activities."[24] Coman's faith encouraged her to believe she would be redeemed through her suffering as Jesus had been. She understood her cancer as a "desecration of the body" that left her spirit uncontaminated. Bates, however, notes that faith did not offer Coman any means or hope of restoring that body: "She prayed to God to spare her one bitter cup after another. . . . God spared her nothing. . . .When God hurt her most, she trusted Him most." Nowhere in Bates's narrative is there even a hint that Coman believed her illness had been inflicted on her as punishment for some female transgression. She may not have understood the connection between God's will and her own suffering but she does not turn this mystery against herself. Unlike many of her contemporaries (and ours), she expresses no guilt and asks no forgiveness for becoming ill.

We do not know what kind of intimacy Bates and Coman shared in their "Boston marriage" (whether sexual or not), but we do know that such relationships were socially acceptable, at least until the time of Coman's death. In the early twentieth century, women's sexuality was still defined exclusively in relation to men. Outside that context, women were considered to be asexual. For those who shunned marriage, living with another woman left them sexually pure. Given the "innocence" of their relationship (before the advent of "deviant," that is, lesbian sex), Coman and Bates would have little reason to feel stigmatized by their devotion to each other. In this sense, they were lucky; Coman's breast cancer was just a disease, neither a sign of God's disfavor nor a mark of shame.

Nonetheless, Bates had difficulties mirroring Coman's convictions. She wanted to align herself with Coman and willed herself to set aside the mental images of her physical torment. "In His will was her peace," Bates declares in her introduction, setting a path for herself. "As I look back on Katharine's martyrdom, I see no longer pain and death; I see only the shining of her spirit." In the pages

21

that follow, she tries to live up to this intention, to let Coman's spirit take precedence over the horror of her suffering.

For anyone accustomed to latter-day illness narratives, Bates's chronicle of disease and death may seem markedly disembodied. Even though nurses were employed to take care of Coman's wounds and renew her dressings, Bates must have seen the full extent of her friend's injuries. Over all this, she draws a veil. The fact that a breast has been removed is never mentioned. Nor is there any reference to the loss of movement and muscle control in the arm on the affected side that was a common and crippling side effect of this surgery. Running parallel to Bates's reserve with the physical details is a similar lack of specifics with regard to medical treatments. This stands in stark contrast to today's familiarity with a wide spectrum of medical therapies and their arcane lexicons, ranging, in the case of breast cancer, from aromatase inhibitors to sentinel nodes. Breast cancer has become a topic that is universally acceptable to speak about in every public forum as well as private gathering. By contrast, Bates's world was one of utter silence on the subject; it is unlikely that she ever saw the words "breast cancer" in print.

Given the absence of any national conversation

about the disease, it is not surprising that Bates never names it. Nor does she identify "the powerful medicine which [Coman] had been taking to prevent recurrence of her trouble." What might read in today's context as diffidence or disinterest is more accurately viewed, at least in part, as a reflection of the very limited exchange of information that took place between physicians and their patients early in the twentieth century. Without any basic medical or scientific understanding to begin with, women patients did not know what questions to ask. Nor did they know how to challenge their doctors' decisions, especially when life-threatening illnesses were at issue. They accepted medical advice more as an instruction than a recommendation.

Despite these limitations, Bates manages to insert into her narrative more than one mention of an occasion when the physician treating Coman misdiagnosed a symptom or misjudged her prognosis. These are presented without any criticism, but that they are included at all must be seen, in retrospect, as daring. On a visit in April 1914 to the celebrated William Sampson Handley nine months before Coman's death, Bates observes that "he made a surface examination (not, as I remember, using the stethoscope) and pronounced her

well. Katharine told him of the pains but he . . .
ascribed them to rheumatism." Of course, he was
wrong.

The relative poverty of treatment options available to Coman, compared to today's extensive
arsenal, has the curious benefit of allowing the
medical side of her story to be pushed into the
background. This helps bring "the shining of her
spirit" to the fore. Most breast cancer narratives
written in the past twenty years are, by contrast,
rooted in the body rather than the spirit. They are
structured by the sequence of interventions into
that body—from biopsy through surgery, radiation,
chemotherapy, etc. Over each of these therapeutic
episodes hovers a different team of doctors who
become major characters in the drama.

Such a format—following a detailed plan with
a road map and a clear set of markers—was obviously not available to Bates. Its absence brings the
more hopeful side of Coman's ordeal into sharper
relief, highlighting periods of convalescence and
the bittersweet moments of recaptured normalcy.
This yields a gentler story that reads more as a
human drama than a medical one. References to
doctors are vastly outnumbered by references to
well-meaning friends. Most important, perhaps,
keeping the disease out of the limelight allows

Bates to showcase the spiritual struggle that Coman could win, rather than the physical battle she
could not. The survival of Coman's faith to the very
end, against heavy odds, enables her to die, as Bates
puts it, "still with her own dignity, her own reserve
upon her." It is the portrayal of this "victory" that
may be the ultimate purpose of Bates's narrative,
crafted as a final act of devotion.

Perhaps it is not surprising, then, that the details of Coman's illness have, like her body after
death, been "cleaned up" for eternity. On the other
hand, the immediacy of that death for Bates is
made apparent in her depiction of Coman's final
hours. Here the narrative shifts tone, moving from
what is largely a summary of the three years leading up to Coman's death to an intimate re-creation
of the deathbed scene itself. The forward motion of
Bates's narrative also comes to a stop and description gives way to dialogue. The language the two
women adopt for their farewells is, for the most
part, not their own, but drawn from the literary
and scriptural canons that have kept them company throughout their lives. Their final appearance
at the death bed echoes earlier, happier occasions
when the two women enjoyed the private exchange
of feelings released by familiar words carried on a
familiar voice. Prayers, psalms, Christina Rossetti,

25

and John Greenleaf Whittier, the sacred and secular, mixed together and, freighted with shared meaning, pass tenderly between them, with each picking up where the other falters. This interweaving of texts persists to the very end when Bates attempts a stanza from Rossetti:

> "Shall not the Judge of all the earth do right?
> Yea, Lord, altho' Thou say me nay . . . "
> I could not say it beyond the first line, but
> Katharine's loyal voice went on: "Yea, Lord."
> As I remember, she did not speak again.

The spiritual connotations of the selected fragments of verse and poems the women shared, together with their rhythmic cadences, provide a kind of coded comfort that served as a substitute for more direct and intimate speech.

POSTMORTEM

After Coman's death, Bates often returned to her love for Coman in her poetry. Gathered into a volume she called *Yellow Clover: A Book of Remembrance*, these poems have an emotional intensity that distinguishes them from most of her other work. In a final section called "In Bohemia: A Corona of Sonnets," named for Coman's old room

at the top of the Scarab, Bates revisits, again and
again, Coman's suffering and death and her own
helplessness in the face of this formidable disease:

> Your only moan:"My soul is among lions."[25]
> You were on shipboard, sailing home to die.
> I sat beside you on the deck; the sky
> Glistened with constellations, starry scions
> Of an eternal fire. Not white-hot irons
> Could so have seared my spirit as that cry
> From your deep anguish.

The poem put her directly back in touch with the
spiritual conflict she had held in check in the days
immediately following Coman's death, when she
crafted a memorial to please Coman rather than
herself. The more peremptory handling of this
theme in the posthumous poems— "One touch of
you were worth a thousand creeds"—reveals just
how thin was the veneer of Bates's Christian resignation. Although she had certainly pushed the
limits of the memorial tribute, admitting a much
wider range of emotional response, shifting perspectives, and a broader canvas of character and
incident, her narrative still remains, ultimately, du-
ty-bound. Poetry released her from the constraints
of formal obligations owed to her subject and to

27

the wider audience of women whose collective grief her tribute had honored. It opened the door to a bleaker, more personal anguish.

Poem after poem in *Yellow Clover* speaks of the loss of Coman. Bates's "faltering faith" and her resistance to the consolations of religious orthodoxy never abate and, in time, seem to encompass an immunity to the consolations of language itself—for a poet, the ultimate hell. In the last stanza of a poem originally titled "Church of the Pointed Firs," Bates confesses:

> Broken by grief, I cannot bear
> The ministry of words;
> Content to taste the sacrament
> Of winds and leaves and birds.[26]

Yellow Clover was finished and published in 1922. The poems reveal that Bates's memories of Coman's illness—"Those four years beset with wasting pain, / The surgeon's knife again and yet again"—still remained fresh years later. So, too, was her memory of Coman's final moments and the last earthly exchange between them through the words of Christina Rossetti: "Words of hers rose faint / From your pale lips, the last ere silence fell."

room as Coman, at the top of the Scarab, listening to John Greenleaf Whittier, read to her by a
friend—just as she herself had recited Whittier to
Coman fourteen years earlier.

2 ❧
"For Katharine Coman's Family and Innermost Circle of Friends"

Because it fell to me, in the friendship which remains my joy and blessing, to know the successive stages of Katharine's long suffering, I would like to set down, in simplest fashion and only for the eyes of those who have love's right to see, the history of her illness. Not for the illness itself; it would have been intolerable to watch the slow destruction of that beautiful body had it not been for the victory of soul. Katharine had always expected of her body wholesomeness and strength, assured that surgery and inward, stealthy, devouring disease would never come to her. Even last June she wrote me from New York that the one thing she could not bear would be a wasting, painful illness.

She had them all to bear,—everything that

This memoir, written in 1915, first appeared in print in *Legacy: A Journal of Women Writers* 23/1 (2006).

was most abhorrent to her nature. She prayed God to spare her one bitter cup after another; she seconded her prayers with the finest and firmest endeavors toward the regaining of health. Her efforts were all in vain; no miracle was wrought for her; God spared her nothing.

And through it all her Christian faith, which in Katharine was one with faithfulness, never faltered. When God hurt her most, she trusted Him most. In His will was her peace. As I look back on Katharine's martyrdom, I see no longer pain and death; I see only the shining of her spirit.

Katharine's glory of health and vigor, her abounding, glad vitality, seemed so essentially herself that I was slow to recognize the first approaches of illness. In 1905 I began to be troubled by her severe and exhausting headaches, but I thought she was only tired and that our open-air summer in England, in 1906, would set her right again. Throughout that holiday summer, however, she showed such serious evidences of nervous strain that my anxieties began in earnest. Her physician suggested an operation, but thought it might safely be postponed, hoping that meanwhile nature would remedy the difficulty, and Katharine went on with her work as simply as if nothing were amiss. Her most important book, *The Economic*

Beginnings of the Far West, was joyfully and persistently wrought out, through travel, study and writing, during years which by many women would have been given over to wretched invalidism.

The operation, which had become imperative, took place at the Newton Hospital, June 1, 1911. The decision was a sudden one. Katharine's college courses were already announced for the coming year. The book on which she had worked so earnestly and long, against such odds, was not quite finished. But she put all her cherished plans aside and, knowing that the chances hung evenly between life and death, faced her ordeal with a tranquil courage that had cost her, however, many a secret battle. A physician consulted in Chicago had made the mistake, carried away by scientific enthusiasm, of showing her colored diagrams illustrating every phase of the critical surgery involved, and those pictures, with their suggestion of the desecration of the body, gave Katharine "a nightmare week." But strengthened, as she believed, by her dear mother, who had died that spring, she commended her spirit and was as cheerfully serene, on the morning of the operation, as she had ever been. She dreaded death only for the grief it would bring to those who loved her. "But I should not leave you comfortless," she wrote just before she went to the table. "I would come to you as my mother comes to me in my best moments when my heart is open to her."

The operation proved successful, and the long, weary convalescence, first at Miss Cornelia Warren's beautiful home, Cedar Hill in Waltham,[29] and then in a rented cottage at Twin Lake, New Hampshire, was made far easier by the deft and tender ministrations of her niece Carol. Sigurd and I were with them there, and in September came Miss Warren. Katharine returned to the Scarab at the end of that month. All the while she was working, as she could, on *The Economic Beginnings of the Far West*, which was ready for the press when she sailed with her brother Seymour, early in January, 1912, for a recuperative trip in Egypt. In making her goodbye call on Dr. Raymond[30] she had intended to speak of something which, with characteristic reticence, she had not mentioned to me nor to anyone,—a tiny lump that had recently appeared in her left breast. If she had done so, she might be within touch and sight of our love today, but interest in some impersonal topic of conversation carried her thought so far from herself that she was out on the ocean before she remembered her omission. A fall in Aswan perhaps made matters worse. She greatly enjoyed the trip and confidently expected to resume her long-interrupted college work in the autumn. She wrote from the steamer: "1 shall be glad to be at home and at work once more. My desk in Bohemia seems a pleasant prospect and it is good to have a congenial task ahead of me."[31] Yet when she returned in April, she brought with her a hidden pain, that grew more insistent week by week and finally drove her, May 28, to consult Dr. Raymond. Supposing she was off with Sigurd, as usual, for a morning run, I was writing in the study, happy in the belief that Katharine was gaining strength from month to month and on the way to recover the radiant health of her birthright. I do not know what it was in the sound of her footsteps on the south porch that struck like a blow on my heart and told me everything. "The hospital again!" I exclaimed, meeting her in the hall. "And when did you turn clairvoyant?" she answered, laughing, but so pale that all her wrong, affectionate design of keeping this new disaster from me was shattered.

The second operation, which we still hoped would be but a slight affair, took place, again at the Newton hospital, June 5, and proved not only very serious in itself but more ominous than we could let her know. "The future will be short and troubled," one of the surgeons said to me, speaking only too truly. During the following days, as I would sit by her hospital bedside reading to her from the proof sheets of the Economic Beginnings, her efforts to hide her pain were heroic. She had wonderful ways, too, of baffling her physical distress. One night when the suffering was at its keenest she concentrated her thoughts on the family problem of a friend and worked out what proved to be a most satisfactory solution.

Again she went from the hospital to Cedar Hill and, after the hub-bub of Commencement was well over, came home with an attendant to the Scarab, where she enjoyed visits from her sister and from her brother Seymour, who had immediately, on hearing the result of the operation, returned from abroad to help her in any way he could. It was during this summer that, lying for hours at a time, in weakness and pain, on the straw couch on our south piazza and observing the unshepherded ways of the little children who abound upon our hill, she conceived the plan and, with her first revival of strength, undertook the enterprise of a town Kindergarten, which became a fact that very winter. The idea was taken up by stray friends, but it was Katharine who first enlisted them. The original Kindergarten is now housed in a model new building on the edge of the college grounds and three similar Kindergartens are maintained in other quarters of Wellesley.[32]

Miss Hazard had sent from Santa Barbara a generous birthday gift for a motor trip, and trains and boats were so contrary that this seemed the best way, all things considered, of getting Katharine, after the middle of August, to North Brooklin, on the Maine coast, opposite Bar Harbor. Her left arm still pained her, but I found a way of supporting it so as to protect it from the jolts and we had four days of swift, sunny air and racing scenery. Katharine gained so much in "that abode of peace," as she called it, under the devoted care of her hostess, Miss Emily Balch, that she hardly understood why we all insisted on her permanent resignation from Wellesley. She yielded to our persuasions, however, and retired on a Carnegie pension.[33] She returned to the Scarab in mid-September and on October 7 we had an impromptu household festival to celebrate the arrival of the first copy of the *Economic Beginnings of the Far West*. A few days later, in the midst of her eager plans for a visit to her La Grange home, with an elaborate schedule of addresses, most carefully worked out, in behalf of the International Institute for Girls in Spain, Katharine suddenly came down with a sharp attack of bronchitis and continued very ill for a month. Her broken plans hurt her more than the cough, which persisted far into the winter and, in view of the mortal peril ever threatening her lungs, kept my anxiety alert.

She busied herself that winter with the preparation of the beautiful book, which her brother Seymour was to print, in memory of their mother, Martha Seymour Coman.[34] He came on in the Christmas holidays and they completed arrangements for the press. At the beginning of May Katharine went west for two happy months at La Grange, the central event being the wedding of her niece Katharine. Just before she left Wellesley, the college faculty gave her a farewell dinner, where the cordial, appreciative speeches in her honor were crowned by a simple, impersonal, noble-thoughted address from herself that lifted the mood of the hour to heights of vision and consecration.

We sailed from New York July 3 for Norway, where Katharine, as later that summer in Sweden, Denmark and Belgium, put the most determined energy into the investigation of Social Insurance problems.[35] All the time her nerves were on the rack and only by repeated victories of self-control was she able to bear the inevitable annoyances and fatigues of travel. Dr. Bainbridge, who saw her in London in October and cheered us by his favorable report and hopeful outlook, said that the powerful medicine which she had been taking to prevent recurrence of her trouble was "tearing the nerves to pieces" and advised her to give it up which she did. We spent the winter in southern Spain, Katharine always working at high pressure and accomplishing wonders. We had many delightful explorations, however, on foot and by carriage, and quiet evening hours of reading, and by spring she was looking well and bonny and really seemed to be recovering nervous tone. We took over a month for the return trip from Seville to Paris, journeying up the picturesque east coast of Spain, and she was almost her old adventurous self again. Ever since December, however, there had been intermittent pains low in the left side. The doctor thought they were rheumatic, and Katharine ignored them as much as possible. These pains came upon her with such severity in Paris that she herself, in her silent way, feared the worst. Miss Olga Halsey,[36] who was helping her there in the Social Insurance inquiries, while I had gone on to London for work of my own, received the impression on Good Friday that Katharine, through the solemn service of the day, was consecrating herself for death. She re-joined me in London April 25 and, to my surprise,—for I had expected to have to use all manner of argument and entreaty,—was more

than ready to see the expert, Dr. Sampson Ha
whom Dr.Bainbridge had advised her to con
the spring.[37] We secured an appointment for
27, when he made a surface examination (no
remember, using the stethoscope) and pronou
her well. Katharine told him of the pains b
too, ascribed them to rheumatism.

We sped back to our lodgings on wings
Katharine, so glad to live and labor, went ard
about her arrangements for a summer of S
Insurance studies in Germany. She threw he
with zest even into shopping and dressmak
We indulged in a little extravagance of recreat
theatre-going and motoring, often accompanie
our friends Mrs. Scofield and her daughter C
But the pains in the left side kept growing wo
Meanwhile the London weather was atroci
and we both took to coughing, like everybody e
Katharine went twice into the country for pure
intending each time a long stay but returning i
day or two to our cozy little hearth, declaring th
the country was colder and wetter than Lond
itself. We called in a local physician, a Scotchma
who gave us tonics and advised us to go, for a r
ally genial climate, to Edinburgh. By the latter pa
of May Katharine was having terrible paroxysm
of coughing, and her breathing at night was lik

that of a child with the croup. When it reached the point where a flight of stairs or an easy walk set her panting, I knew we were in grave trouble, but could by no persuasion induce her to go again to Dr. Handley.

On the second of June we received word from home of the death of Sigurd, the golden collie who had been our merry, loving comrade for eleven years. He had his meed of tears, and we were not ashamed of our grief. Sigurd had always a way of running ahead and waiting gleefully to surprise us as we rounded a corner, and his going intensified my fear for Katharine. I had forgotten Dr. Handley's exact address, and she, laughing at my concern, would not give it to me. Leaving our lodgings the next morning as if I were going to the British Museum reading-room, as usual, I went instead to our tourist bank (Brown Shipley), hunted up the address in the London directory and wrote there to Dr. Handley a full account of these recent developments. After dinner that evening I confessed to Katharine, who said never a word. Dr. Handley's reply, stating that the symptoms were significant and alarming and that she should see him at once, was at our breakfast-table the next morning. I set the marmalade-jar on it, but Katharine had seen. She asked me to read the letter aloud and then, without comment, took up the *Times* and gave me the morning news. On June 5, just two years from the date of the second operation, Dr. Handley told us that cancer was at work in the left lung and that Katharine could not live a year.

Again, as so often before, all her plans, so zealously made and so tenaciously held, were suddenly in ruins about her, but within an hour after her sentence had been spoken she was busy at our writing-table, changing steamer-dates, cancelling engagements, resigning her appointments as delegate to two European conferences that summer, informing her nearest friends at home of her immediate return. Miss Warren and Miss McDowall arrived in London that afternoon and we met them at the station and had them over to dinner with us as we had expected. Katharine carried a gallant front through it all. Once, a few days later, I saw traces of tears in those brave eyes, but never again in the seven months that followed.

We sailed June 13, well in advance of any rumors of war and under especially spacious and comfortable conditions. Katharine had kept up, making goodbye calls and giving goodbye teas, attending to the business, as she always liked to do, and even looking after tickets and checks at the station, until we were fairly on board. Then, at last, she was willing to be cared for. All the way over she was very quiet, very natural, but the spiritual struggle was hard. The dread, not of death but of dying, the horror of the treacherous disease that was consuming her body, had taken hold of her. She said: "My soul is among lions."[38]

Her brother Seymour, whose devotion did so much to uphold her through the coming fortnight, and Dr. Mosher, physician to mind as well as to body in that period of sore suspense, were among the friends who met us on landing.[39] In their care and that of Dr. Bainbridge I left her, still with a faint hope which fell before a verdict that confirmed the word of Dr. Handley. Her letters told me tenderly and cheerfully, making the best of the worst and dwelling upon the immediate comforts and alleviations of her situation. "God is taking care of your broken dolly," she wrote July 3 from the Berkshires, and went on to tell how the fresh air was relieving her cough. She had expected to go to her sister at La Grange, eager to see the new little Katharine there, but the journey was too long.[40] Her brother's undaunted perseverance succeeded in discovering ideal summer quarters for her in Lanesboro, within easy motor reach of Pittsfield [Massachusetts], where she could have the electric treatment prescribed.

MY SOUL IS AMONG LIONS

In many ways it was a beautiful summer. Miss Balch and I took turns in being with Katharine and caring for her. Her brother returned in August for a visit of some ten days, and Dr. Mosher, radiating courage and joy, came to her twice, finding her general condition so much improved that we began to hope again. All the summer, notwithstanding the pain that was gnawing in her side, the panting breath and the weakness that made even the few steps to her hammock an exhausting effort, Katharine's bearing was one of unclouded serenity. She had started in on a new book, *The Industrial History of New England*, and was able to read and make notes for it an hour or two a day. She wrote, at first, many letters, usually to intimate friends and above all to her dear home-people; she listened with interest to the books and newspapers that were read to her, and enjoyed all the evidences of love that came flooding in, especially the frequent boxes of oranges from Covina and the snapshots of Little Katharine the Third. In that restful Gloucester hammock, supplied by Miss Balch, she would lie for hours, feeding her eyes and soul on the beauty of the hills. Our hosts, and even the members of their changing summer household, were kindness itself, and Katharine took continual pleasure in the sights and sounds and daily doings of the farm, which seemed to enfold her, this last summer of her life, in the sweet and happy memories of childhood.

The cold weather of early September, confining Katharine to the house, cut short her stay in Lanesboro. Once more she had the joy of a visit with Miss Warren at Cedar Hill. To add to her content, her sister was with her there, and her increasing physical needs were well cared for by a nurse from Lanesboro, Mrs. Kennedy. She came home to the Scarab, with her sister and nurse, September 25. Mr. Coburn came on and, in a few days, his wife returned with him to La Grange. Replacing Mrs. Kennedy, who was called to another case, Miss Mason arrived October first. Her gentle, tactful, self-forgetful devotion never wavered to the end. During the autumn, despite all our efforts, hopes and prayers, Katharine was losing ground. She was able, at first, to drive by motor, once or twice a. week, to Newton Center for the X-ray treatment. She took, besides, several drives for pleasure, trying bravely to ignore the hurt that every jolt gave to that poor left side, which we did our best to protect by cushions. Her condition varied from day to day. She was very ill October sixth, but on October eighth Miss Warren came over with her new electric car and took us both on a delectable red-and-gold woodland drive. Dr. Mosher, always bringing hope and courage with her, came October tenth and found, on examining Katharine the following day, that the left lung was "wonderfully better," but on October fourteenth, in one of her rare admissions of distress, Katharine said to me that she was "so tired of the pain." In the next few days the panting and coughing were only too evidently on the increase. Yet we had an hour's drive through enchanted weather on the fifteenth and a shorter drive on the twenty-second, but when on the twenty-fifth Miss Warren came over to take her for a turn in the "perambulator," Katharine was not well enough to go. Toward the end of the month, though she maintained her tone of tranquil cheerfulness and was still working a little, almost every day, on her new book, she was looking very white and weary. Dr. Raymond, whose unremitting care did everything possible to relieve the various concomitant ills of the disease, suggested that Katharine should go in to the Peter Bent Brigham hospital for observation,—a proposition that her brother, and his medical adviser, Dr. Capps, approved. On All Saints, November first, Mr. Dean administered to her the sacrament of the Lord's Supper.[41] At her desire, her friends Olga Halsey and Miss Florence Converse communed with her. Monday morning we took her in to the hospital by motor and left her to the doctors, whose examinations were exhausting and whose forecasts hopeless.

She was worn out and—even Katharine—all disheartened when we brought her home again on Friday. She nestled down with a thankful sigh into her own bed in her own Bohemia. Not even her unselfish fortitude could hide the suffering in the days next following. As a last hope, we resorted to Dr. Nowell's serum, which was first injected November thirteenth. Katharine and I tried hard to believe it was helping her. On the fourteenth she went on a wee drive, but it made her cough, and on her (57th) birthday, Monday the twenty-third, the day for whose happiness we had all so carefully planned, the pain took her cruelly. She was better again and came down Thursday to a very quiet Thanksgiving dinner, with Mrs. Guild, whom Katharine especially wanted, for our only guest.[42] The next two days the panting and coughing were worse. Her brother came on Sunday and, in the pleasure of his visit, she seemed, for a while, to grow better. She took her last drive with him. On December twelfth she was not so well but Miss Warren was over on Sunday the thirteenth, and Katharine, in her pretty white dress that she wore only once again—in death—, came down to dinner.

She had a hard day Monday, and on Tuesday, when she was downstairs for the last time, the new pain in the right side leapt upon her.

Dr. Raymond spent the evening working over her, and Miss Locke then began her strong, efficient service, maintained to the last, as night-nurse. From this time on morphine was freely used. On Wednesday afternoon Katharine, utterly ill though she was, remembered that I was having my weekly graduate class in the study and sent down roses. Through the latter half of the week she seemed, day by day, to be sinking fast toward death, but her mind was never affected by the opiate and she was always our own Katharine, meeting whatever came with an unshaken Christian trust and loyalty. Once, as I bent over her, she murmured: "God is everything. It is all God." And on another day, as she watched the falling snow: "How white the flakes come down, like the thoughts of God!" She was so weak that she could not lift her head. "It is strange," she said. "My soul aspires, but my body lies here like a log." Very clearly now the soul and body were going different ways, the one shining more and more brightly in beauty and in strength while the other, still so dear, was perishing before our eyes. Dr. Raymond, and the two physicians called in consultation, warned us that the end was probably close at hand. On Saturday night the whole machinery of the chest seemed to creak and rattle with every breath, but on Sunday she was easier, though very, very weak, and received loving little calls from Miss Balch and Miss Warren. Her sister arrived Monday evening and meanwhile the morphine had given the tortured body so deep a rest that the vital forces were once more rallying. Mrs. Coburn found Katharine stronger than the doctors had thought she could ever be again. Tuesday, Wednesday and Thursday she brightened more and more, happy in the soothing presence of her sister, whose choice to spend Christmas with her rather than with the precious family in La Grange she accepted, though a little puzzled at first, as an expression of loving solicitude. The morphine, with its blissful relief from suffering, had raised her spirits and she told Dr. Raymond that, for the first time since June, she felt that she was going to get well.

At times, however, she seemed to understand. On Wednesday evening, December twenty-third, I was in her room just after she had wakened from a brief sleep. It was a happy waking, for she felt, she said, not only no pain but no sense of sickness. She asked me to repeat the Shepherd's Psalm, taking up the phrase when my voice broke in the

Valley-of-the-Shadow verse, and said quietly, at the end: "It is perfectly true,—perfectly true. The words that have come to me over and over these past weeks are: 'I shall not die, but live, and declare the works of the Lord.' I had thought it was a promise for this life, but if it means the life beyond what we call death, it makes no difference.

She said again and again that her Christmas was the most beautiful that she had ever known,—beautiful, most of all, in that her "nearest and dearest" were with her. She was herself the very spirit of Christmas, turning on its interchange of cards and gifts all her old concentration of attention, trying to call every friend to mind and to have her thanks returned for every remembrance. That was no light matter, for from early morning of the twenty-fourth florists' boys and expressmen were bringing to the house from far and near such a wealth of cut flowers and potted plants for her that it was hard to find space for them even in Bohemia. She rejoiced in them all, roses in rich and varied tints, mignonette, lilies of the valley, pansies, carnations, violets, poinsettias, acacia, heather, partridge berries, azaleas white and pink, cyclamen, daffodils, blue browallia, narcissus, Jerusalem cherry, camellia-japonica, ferns, primroses, jonquils and baskets of Christmas greens, and she rejoiced even more in the abounding lovingkindness that they represented. "I used to think," she said, "that I was not fortunate in making friends, but now—." Her sister brought in a great pine-wreath, and Miss Balch a splendid holly-bough. A well-beloved friend and pupil, Nan Scoville, sent a box of fragrant forest sprays, and that indefatigable brother worked hard in putting all these up on the walls in position where they could easily be seen from the bed. Olga Halsey had trimmed a glistening little green and white Christmas tree that stood on the table and all manner of choice and merry gifts were grouped about it. Katharine had the day exactly planned out from dawn to eve—just when we were to come up to open her packages, and just when Mrs. Reddell was to appear with Daisy, most impish of kittens, for whom the impartial Christmas tree had presents of catnip and a mechanical mouse, and just how the dinner,—in which Katharine was greatly interested, though for herself eating, long since distasteful, had now become a task of utmost difficulty,— was to proceed unbroken through its earlier courses before anyone—we each pleaded for the privilege—should leave the table to bring up her tiny portion. After all, we could be with her but little, for the very excitement of her pleasure tired her and she bad to rest much of the day, but her sleep was tranquil and, whenever she woke, she woke amid bloom and fragrance in her own little Paradise that love had made for her in anticipation of the heavenly gardens only a step beyond.

Our Christmas truce with Pain and Death held over Twelfth Night. Katharine, still free from suffering and pathetically glad—so revealing what the brave efforts of the autumn had cost her—to lie still and be at rest, took constant delight in her flowers, in the ministering presence of her brother and sister and in the greetings from friends and from the far-away members of the family. Her thoughts dwelt much upon the California wedding. Letters from Morrie and Ted pleased her greatly, as well as a letter from Ralph, a little neighbor-lad who often asked after "the Lady who took me in to see *The Bluebird*, adding wistfully: "I hope she gets well."[43] The Sunday morning after Christmas Katharine said to me, as I went in for my usual early glimpse: "The night has been so short. It seemed like only midnight when Miss Mason came to my bed this morning. I was sleeping so peacefully. It is not only that the pain is all gone and I am feeling perfectly comfortable. The depression and distress are all gone, too, and I am light-hearted."

During her illness Katharine had developed what she called her sixth sense. Resting alone, as she often preferred to rest, in the stillness of her upper chamber, with the knob of her electric bell in hand so that she could call us by the slightest of exertions, she was nevertheless aware of all the comings and goings of the home. Every footstep on the path or on the porch, every opening and shutting of a door, gave her tidings of us. She listened for Mr. Dean's carriage when he came, on the Monday after Christmas, to administer to her again the rite of Holy Communion. It was a deep satisfaction to her to have her sister with her in that sacrament.

Katharine seemed so much stronger that Dr. Raymond, who for her sake had spent the vacation in Wellesley, tireless in loving devotion, thought that wonderful vitality might resist death some weeks longer. Planning for another coming in the spring, Mrs. Coburn left us on Thursday December thirtieth and Mr. Coman on Sunday January third. Katharine's spirits drooped a little after each goodbye, but her brother spent with her much of the day of Mrs. Coburn's going, and against his departure I had ready a new novel, Dawson's *The Raft*,[44] hoping that the children in it might entertain her, as they did, especially Peter when he was "Peterish." She was interested, too, in the return of my sister, of Olga and of Esther from their Christmas absences and wanted to see them all and welcome them back. She worked eagerly with Olga on Wednesday, hearing and discussing the editor's introduction to Katharine's collected *Survey* articles on Social Insurance, about to be published in pamphlet form as a campaign document of the Progressive Party. Olga came down from Bohemia with glad eyes, saying: "It seemed like old times." But by Thursday night Katharine was not so well. We thought she had perhaps overdone a little or been too ambitious in her attempts to get on with less of the opiate. All day Friday she continued tired and restless, though still, as even on Saturday, she worked for brief half-hours over Social Insurance with Olga. On Saturday morning she owned up to "a little pain in the left side" during the night. Dr. Raymond at once renewed the hypodermics, which again lifted Katharine above the reach of suffering, while not in the least confusing her mind. She interrupted the story-book that afternoon to give me data for several letters in the interests of the International Institute.

On Saturday night the breathing was labored and when I went in early Sunday morning, instead of greeting me with the encouraging word for which, even at her worst, she had seldom sought in vain, Katharine said faintly: "I am weak." She had so little breath to spend in speech that, to keep her from trying to talk, I read to her, with the necessary intervals, hour after hour. Our novel advanced that day from page 196 to page 287, where I put in the mark that will not be moved. I shall never finish that story. Katharine followed it all with amused interest, although disappointed to find that the children were growing up. True to her principle of accomplishing something every day, she made me, in the middle of the afternoon, put the novel down. "We mustn't waste all our time over Peter, especially now that he's falling in love. We must get something done. I want to write my home letters." She dictated a merry little note to her brother Charles, but so gaspingly that, when it came to "Susie's letter," I induced her to give me just the catch-words and let me write it out later. By that time her slender stock of strength was spent. "Seymour's letter," she said, "must wait till morning."

After a little rest, Katharine asked for a psalm and then proposed that we begin one of the Gospels and read it through, a chapter a day. She chose St.Luke, "omitting the Gospel of the Nativity." I began with the fourth chapter and she promptly sent me back to the third, protesting: "You are leaving out the Baptism." I went on for twenty-three verses and then asked: "Do I have to read all this genealogy?" "No," returned Katharine, always so well up in canonical lore. "That is a late addition."

Her meals had become tribulations to her, but this evening supper went almost blithely. Her brother had presented the Scarab with a large electric torch, and we tried the experiment of standing that up on end on her little table, so as to light the tray without troubling her eyes. The device worked well and its novelty entertained her. She took a spoonful or two of buttermilk,—the buttermilk that a steadfast friend since the beginning of her Wellesley life, Miss Mary Willcox, was at great pains to prepare for her and send to her from Newton two or three times a week, and she tasted the champagne I had, on my latest trip to Boston, procured for her,—"K.L.B.'s vagary," as she called it.

Her obvious weakness, and difficulty in getting breath enough, made me anxious, though she did not seem nearly as ill as in that terrible week before Christmas. I went to her door several times during the night, but all was quiet until three o'clock when I heard her chatting "with her nurse in a voice so strong and cheerful that I thought, as was indeed the case, she had been resting well. She had one more comfortable hour, but when I went in, at sunrise, she reached up both her arms to me, with an unwonted, almost childlike appeal, for the help I could not give, saying so brokenly and feebly that I could hardly catch the words: "I woke—at four—with this oppression—on my chest." In a moment she continued, with her habitual effect of reassuring serenity: "But It will pass." She had said to Dr. Raymond the morning before, when asking her for something to help her breathing: "Perhaps it can't be helped and if not, it is all right."

As I lifted the shade that she might enjoy the flush in the sky, I did not yet realize that this pale-rose dawn was the last those dear gray eyes would ever see. Miss Mason was moving softly about, preparing the malted milk, as usual, and when, after dressing, I came back to make sure that Katharine was not left alone, she was taking a few drops of my "vagary," the last nourishment that passed her lips. I was surprised, as I was hurrying back to her after a brief breakfast, to meet Dr. Raymond, whom Miss Locke had called by telephone, on the stairs. Dr. Raymond told me that the end was close at hand, and for the hour and a half that remained, I was beside Katharine, who did not seem, until perhaps at the very last, to know that she was dying.

In October Cornelia Warren had given her, the "friend of many years, with love that outlasts years," a little book of "Prayers Ancient and Modern," and

75

ever since, even on the crowded mornings when I had to be in my classroom at nine, I would read her the prayer for the day and one of the psalms she loved so well. So this morning, as always, we had our little service. Katharine listened to the prayer for January eleventh and echoed "Amen," but asked me to read again "yesterday's prayer," which had brightened her face when first she heard it and which she called for a second time Sunday afternoon. So I read:

"Let me not seek out of Thee what I can find only in Thee, O Lord, peace and rest and joy and bliss, which abide only in Thine abiding joy. Lift up my soul above the weary round of harassing thoughts to Thy eternal Presence. Lift up my soul to the pure, bright, serene, radiant atmosphere of Thy Presence, that there I may breathe freely, there repose in Thy love, there be at rest from myself and from all things that weary me; and thence return, arrayed with Thy peace, to do and bear what shall please Thee.—Amen."

And again she echoed: "Amen."

"What psalm this morning, Darling?" "The one-hundred-and-third."

And I marvelled, even then, at the high honor with which she kept the faith, her unswerving allegiance, the greatness and devoutness of her soul that in extremity of mortal weakness, with every earthly prayer denied, would still "bless the Lord."

What with stress of feeling and the effort to hold my voice steady, I repeated the psalm incorrectly, throwing some of the verses out of sequence. Katharine heard me with forbearance to the end and then said:

"Now get the book—and *read* it—RIGHT."

At the end of the psalm, whose closing words Katharine murmured after me, Dr. Raymond came in with Miss Mason and injected morphia once more.

"I am stronger now," said Katharine, and her voice, low as it was, had the old reassuring note.

With Dr. Raymond sitting at one side of the bed, near the window, and with me in my accustomed place at the other, Katharine lay quiet, breathing faintly, but still in control of the situation. As Dr. Raymond moved the fan or touched the dry lips with water, Katharine would indicate whether she wanted less or more. It had been arranged on Sunday afternoon that Mr. Dean was to come over this morning for an early service. Katharine remembered the arrangement and spoke of it several times. Olga telephoned Mr. Dean, who was planning to arrive at ten. As Katharine felt herself growing weaker, she said, as she had said on previous occasions before these services: "Ask Mr. Dean—be brief." We assented and in a moment she added, mindful, as always, of practical detail: "Hold the carriage."

Dr. Raymond had partly lowered the shades, so that Katharine might more readily fall asleep and we both were careful not to call her attention nor rouse her from the merciful rest into which she was now sinking fast; but whenever she turned her head a little toward me, as she did from time to time, I would respond with such words of love and faith as were most familiar,—often with Scripture text or stanza of some poem we both knew well. She had by heart many of the sacred lyrics of Christina Rossetti and I repeated the first stanza of one we had often said together in the summer twilights at Lanesboro.

O mine enemy,
Rejoice not over me!
Jesus waiteth to be gracious;
I shall yet arise,
Mounting free and far
Past sun and star,
To a house prepared and spacious
In the skies.

Not sure that she was following, I paused, and Katharine, in a voice so husky and broken that at first I did not understand, took up the next stanza and carried it into the third line, when I resumed it.

> Lord, for Thine own sake,
> Kindle my heart and break:
> Make mine anguish efficacious
> Wedded to Thine own:
> Be not Thy dear pain,
> Thy Love, in vain,
> Thou Who waited to be gracious
> On Thy throne.[45]

A little later, she turned her face once more toward me and tried to smile. The muscles did not entirely obey, but all the meaning of the smile was there,—courage, love, cheer and, it seemed to me, knowledge.

She had often, in health, said she wished to be told when she was dying, and I tried to tell her in stanzas from Whittier which had become, in these last months, a part of our common intercourse.

> I know not where His islands lift
>   Their fronded palms in air;
> I only know I cannot drift
>   Beyond His love and care.

And so beside the Silent Sea
   I wait the muffled oar;
No harm from Him can come to me
   On Ocean as on shore.[46]

She seemed to understand and acquiesce, and I attempted a stanza from Christina Rosetti which I knew would be to her, if she could hear it, fully significant. The stanza runs:

Shall not the Judge of all the earth do right?
   Yea, Lord, altho' Thou say me nay.
Shall not His Will be to me life and light?
   Yea, Lord, altho' Thou slay.

I could not say it beyond the first line, but Katharine's loyal voice went on:
   "Yea, Lord."

As I remember, she did not speak again.

In her hushed and shadowed Bohemia she lay, breathing more and more faintly, apparently at peace, still with her own dignity, her own reserve upon her, even in dying. The hand I was holding clasped mine closely, but not with any suggestion of distress. The last text, I repeated to her as she sank beyond the reach of human love, was the one she held, perhaps, most precious:

"Underneath are the everlasting arms."[47]

She ceased breathing so gradually, so quietly, that we could not tell the instant—approximately half-past nine—when she entered into the new life.

3 ⚜
An Unsung Heroine: Janet Elizabeth Lane-Claypon

Almost eighty years ago, the British Ministry of Health published the first of several groundbreaking studies investigating the risk factors and the results of surgery for breast cancer. This was the work of an English physician named Janet Elizabeth Lane-Claypon (1877–1967). This remarkable researcher brought an innovative perspective and methodological rigor to the design and analysis of breast cancer surveys that established her as a pioneer of cancer epidemiology. Her primary work in the field was credited as the first major case-control study of a non-infectious disease. But while many of her insights and original contributions have evolved into standard practices, Lane-Claypon herself has been wholly effaced from the

Written with the epidemiologist Warren Winkelstein, Jr., this article first appeared in the May–June 2004 issue of the Breast Cancer Action newsletter..

mainstream historical record.

Born in 1877 to a well-to-do family in Lincoln-shire and educated privately at home, Lane-Clay-pon enrolled at the London School of Medicine for Women in 1898. By 1910, Lane-Claypon had acquired student honors, distinctive fellowships, and a string of degrees, including a doctorate in physiology and an M.D. She first put these skills to work in the research lab, investigating the biochemistry of milk and aspects of reproductive physiology, including, importantly, the structure and function of the ovary and the hormonal con-trol of lactation. All of those studies would later inform her thinking on the epidemiology of breast cancer.

She moved from the lab to the arena of public health, where she grappled with a variety of mater-nal and child health issues. She became an advo-cate for breast feeding, as well as for the reform of midwife training and prenatal services, with a view to reducing the number of premature births and stillbirths and the rate of maternal mortality.

In 1923, the minister of health, Neville Cham-berlain, set up a committee to look into the "causa-tion, prevalence and treatment of cancer" and to advise the ministry on the best way to investigate these problems. Lane-Claypon was hired to review the existing literature on breast cancer with an emphasis on its surgical treatment which was primarily the radical mastectomy. The committee then commissioned her to undertake a larger study "with a sufficient and suitable series" of women with breast cancer histories and "a parallel and equally representative series of control cases," that is, "women whose conditions of life were broadly comparable to those of the cancer series but who had no sign of cancer."

No large-scale review of this kind had ever been undertaken. Lane-Claypon realized that to generate a sufficient number of cases and controls—five hundred in each category—she would need to enlist the support of several hospitals. Ultimately, six London and three Glasgow hospitals contributed data to the study, much of it apparently gathered under the supervision of other women physicians. Cases were defined as either recent or currently treated patients with breast cancer. Controls, women with no current or past histories of cancer, were drawn from inpatient and outpatient services of the hospitals supplying the cases. To demonstrate their comparability, Lane-Claypon evaluated both groups with respect to several variables, including occupation and infant mortality (both taken as proxies for social status), nationality, marital status, and age.

The detailed survey that emerged constituted, as far as we know, the first published epidemiological questionnaire. Among the more than 50 questions it asked were several relating to the respondents' reproductive health histories. This yielded results that enabled Lane-Claypon to identify many of the risk factors for breast cancer that are still considered valid today. Her conclusions (or her data reworked by later researchers) agreed with those of modern reviewers: breast cancer was associated with age at menopause, artificial menopause, age at first pregnancy (age at marriage used as a proxy), number of children, and lactation.

In 1926, the Ministry of Health published another Lane-Claypon report that is now considered the first "end results" study. It followed a large sample of women with pathologically confirmed breast cancer for up to ten years after their surgery. The study confirmed that women who were surgically treated at an early stage of the disease had a much better chance of surviving three, five, or ten years longer than those operated on at any later stage.

Woven through all of these reports are Lane-Claypon's scrupulous and prescient concerns about the drawbacks and uncertainties that her own methodology exposed. Sidebar discussions reveal an extraordinarily rigorous and subtle intelligence at work. In the end-results study just mentioned, Lane-Claypon acknowledges the difficulties involved in deriving an accurate staging of the disease (in the days before routine diagnostic biopsies). She understood that differences in access to health care (and hence to surgical treatment) would influence survival results. She recognized the problems of bias created by limiting the study to survivors and by relying on the recall of breast cancer patients themselves rather than observing (with greater neutrality and potentially greater accuracy) the experience of newly diagnosed women going through treatment and beyond. Finally, in reviewing the family histories of her cases, she anticipated the role that genes might play in the development of breast cancer. "There appear to be some families," she wrote, "in which for reasons not certain at present, cancer plays havoc with the members, and there is (some) slight evidence in some instances that it attacks the same organs."

In short, she opened up the field to a host of important and wide-ranging considerations that would be taken up gradually by generations of epidemiologists. Alas, she didn't stay on to share her wisdom directly with those coming up behind her. Shortly after the publication of her landmark cancer studies, having published thirty scientific reports and three books, Lane-Claypon married a colleague at the Ministry of Health and, facing an unforgiving Civil Service Marriage Bar, retired to be a country wife until her death almost forty years later. The abrupt end to her career not only denied her the opportunity to mentor the next generation and, especially, to serve as a powerful role model for women but also interrupted the dissemination and development of her own ideas. Withdrawing from the field with no heir apparent or protégés in place to carry on inevitably consigned her career to obscurity, denying her membership in that elite group of breast cancer pioneers to which she so rightly belongs.

4

Irma Natanson and the Legal Landmark *Natanson v. Kline*

The breast cancer battlefield is littered with desperate remedies.[48] And, at least until quite recently, every one of them was first tried out on women who had little or no idea they were serving as guinea pigs. These women were doubly unlucky: first, to be diagnosed with breast cancer, and second, to have their diagnoses coincide with the introduction of a new and unproven therapy. Whether a genuinely new treatment or a recycled version of an existing one, it would remain experimental at best while women put their bodies on the line to test the new hypothesis. Until evidence could be gathered and assessed, these women were as much experimental "subjects" as they were patients.

The timing of Irma Natanson's breast cancer

This article appeared in the Fall 2004 issue of the Breast Cancer Action newsletter.

diagnosis was unfortunate in the extreme. Her entry into the world of medical treatment in 1955, as a thirty-five-year-old housewife and mother in Wichita, Kansas, coincided almost exactly with the entry of cobalt radiotherapy into the treatment arsenal. Introduced a few years earlier in Canada but still untested in the United States, the "cobalt bomb" had the capacity to penetrate deeper into the body with less skin injury than that typically inflicted by x-rays. The amount of cobalt irradiation that could be administered was governed by the tolerance of the tissues lying five millimeters below the surface of the skin. But there was no way of determining what those tolerance levels would be without the critical feedback provided—unknowingly—by the first generation of patients.

Natanson was a member of this involuntary vanguard, one of the first patients in Kansas, if not in the country, to undergo cobalt treatment. Her surgeon recommended this treatment even though tissue examined after her radical mastectomy revealed no lymph node involvement, and the subsequent removal of her ovaries and fallopian tubes showed no spread to those organs either.

The results were disastrous. The treatment left her with permanent disabilities that seriously compromised her health and the quality of her life, denying her any hope of a return to normalcy. She suffered massive burns that caused enormous pain, smelled bad, and refused to heal. She lost the use of her left lung, which gave rise to chronic wheezing.

Natanson spent a year in a Missouri hospital undergoing more than twenty plastic surgeries—blood vessel and scar repairs, skin grafts, and more—to promote the healing and restoration of her upper body. Some of those procedures further aggravated her injuries. They cut off the blood supply to her arm and left it pinned to the side of her body, rendering it lifeless. Many years later, surgeons at the Mayo Clinic tried to restore the use of her arm by separating it from the side of her body and reactivating its blood supply, but they failed to achieve the desired results. Over time, gangrene developed in her hand and she had to have some fingers amputated. As a pianist, Natanson found this especially hard to bear.

Adding insult to injury, Natanson and her family faced enormous medical bills. Decades before the advent of comprehensive health insurance, many treatment costs fell squarely on the patient. From some extraordinary reserve of resilience and courage (and perhaps even a sense of unspoken outrage), Natanson made the decision to sue for damages, charging that her radiologist, Dr. John R. Kline, had failed to inform her of the hazards of cobalt radiation and had denied that "the treatment involved any danger whatever."[49]

The legal case that ensued, *Natanson v. Kline*, was a landmark in many respects. For perhaps the first time in a public arena, the case exposed, quite literally, the horrific damage done to women's bodies by prevailing breast cancer treatments. Natanson's attorneys proposed to reveal before the jury the full extent of her injuries. The judge closed the courtroom to the public, drew the curtains and, according to one of the attorneys present, Irma Natanson "bared herself to the waist and all could see the injury...the ribs had been destroyed by the radiation and the best that [reconstructive surgery] had been able to accomplish, was to have a layer of skin over the opening. I recall seeing the beat of the heart reflected in movements of this skin flap."

The distress this caused Natanson is hard to imagine, but there could have been no more compelling evidence for the jury to consider. What woman would knowingly submit to treatment that would so harrow and mutilate her?

The failure of Natanson's radiologist to warn her of the risks of cobalt treatment inevitably opened up the legal discussion of "informed

consent." Though *Natanson v. Kline* did not introduce the term itself, it provided the first working
definition of the doctrine, setting a precedent that
the courts would rely on for more than a decade.

Justice Shroeder ruled for the Kansas Su-
preme Court that physicians had "the obligation…
to disclose and explain to the patient in language
as simple as necessary the nature of the ailment,
the probability of success or of alternatives, and
perhaps the risks of unfortunate results and un-
foreseen conditions with the body."

Unfortunately, the issue of whether and how
much information a physician should disclose
to a patient came smack up against a deeply entrenched paternalism, which held that doctors
could be trusted to make decisions in their patients' best interests. The similarities in the relationships between lawyers and their clients on the
one hand, and that between doctors and patients
on the other, were not lost on the judges in this or
any other case reviewing informed consent. All of
them were reluctant to trespass into territory held
to be professionally inviolable. Shroeder was so
anxious to avoid stepping on the toes of his fel-
low professionals that, in his written opinion, he
backed away from his strong move in the direction
of patients' rights and chose instead to reinforce

the ultimate decision-making power of the physician. "The duty of the physician to disclose, however, is limited to those disclosures that a reasonable medical practitioner would make under the same or similar circumstances. How the physician may best discharge his obligation to the patient in this difficult situation involves primarily a question of medical judgment," he wrote.

And, the court added, medical judgment could extend to whatever infantilizing prevarications the physician chose to employ. The ruling stated, "There is probably a privilege, on therapeutic grounds, to withhold the specific diagnosis where the disclosure of cancer... would seriously jeopardize the recovery of an unstable, temperamental or severely depressed patient."

The court, in the end, could not figure out how to grant more decision-making power to the patient without taking it away from her physician. The ambivalence expressed here would continue to plague the discussion of informed consent for decades.

Nonetheless, the decision represented a significant—if limited—step along the path toward patient decision making. And the court did award sufficient damages to Natanson to cover her medical costs. The courageous Irma Natanson survived in her compromised state for another thirty years. Very late in her life she confided to her nephew that she could "still smell her burnt bone and burnt skin. I am still smoldering." In 1989, she was diagnosed with another cancer of unknown origin. By the time it was discovered, it had already spread throughout her body and she died just a few months later.

Almost fifty years after Natanson's original diagnosis, breast cancer has become the most common cause of medical malpractice claims. Although radiation treatment has now become much safer, radiologists appear more often than other specialists in these lawsuits. Now, however, they are charged not with mistreating their patients but with misdiagnosing them.[50] Three of every four claims brought against them result in an award for the plaintiff.

5 ❧
Barbie Meets Breast Cancer

Ruth Handler was the CEO and co-founder, with her husband, of the hugely successful Mattel Toy Company. In the late 1950s she became the driving force behind the design, development, and marketing of what would become Mattel's perennial cash cow, the infamous Barbie Doll.

Named after Handler's own daughter, Barbie was the first doll to have breasts. But on Barbie's very skinny body, these breasts were distinctly outsized, generating expectations of an adolescent body type among little girls that in reality were virtually unattainable. Handler, at least publicly, defended the breasts and ignored the body, emphasizing the self-esteem she believed girls would develop in anticipating the arrival of breasts in their teenage years and acknowledging the role they would inevitably play in determining their mature self-image.

This article appeared in the September 2005 issue of the Breast Cancer Action newsletter.

In this "mammocentric" universe populated by Barbies of her own making, Handler's breast cancer diagnosis and the subsequent loss of a breast seem a curious bit of corporal karma. Handler, however, would not take it lying down. Not only was she driven to find an acceptable replacement for her own loss, she found a way to make it pay, marketing a new line of improved breast prostheses for other women in her situation. She even managed to spin a seamless web, fixing the breast at the center of her life's work. As she explained to a reporter in a carefully crafted sound bite, "When I conceived Barbie, I believed it was important to a little girl's self-esteem to play with a doll that has breasts. Now I find it even more important to return that self-esteem to women who have lost theirs."[51]

Handler underwent several breast biopsies over more than a decade; four times the results came back negative. Then, in 1970, a genuine malignancy turned up and she decided to undergo a modified radical mastectomy. The pain and post-operative depression that ensued caught her off guard. She decided to search for a breast prosthesis to help restore a sense of normalcy, but she found only "heavy shapeless globs that plop into either side of your bra cup, and then sag and shift." (Note that these early breast forms also lacked nipples, as did

Barbie.) Disappointed, Handler went straight to a prosthesis designer and asked him to fit her with a custom breast form. It then occurred to her that there were thousands of women like herself whose lives could be significantly brightened by the availability of properly fitting, comfortable, and affordable prostheses. She could meet their desperate need with products of her own. No longer CEO of Mattel, having been forced out following a mail fraud scandal, she was in a good position to set up a company of her own. Opening for business in 1976, the new enterprise soon began trading its line of prostheses under the brand Nearly Me.[52]

To this new venture, Handler brought the same acumen and marketing skills that had served her well at Mattel. Most of all, she brought herself. She took on grueling promotional tours that, at department stores and even on television, featured Ruth Handler opening her blouse, exposing her bra and asking the audience to guess which cup held the natural breast and which the prosthesis. (A photo of this demonstration appeared in People magazine in 1977.) As a marketing strategy in the late 1970s, this was definitely pushing the envelope.

In early ads for the new line, Handler claimed that Nearly Me offered the "world's first separately designed and contoured left and right breasts" and

99

the "world's only bra-sized breast prostheses from 34B to 40D." Considerable research and development (R&D) had, in fact, been carried out by a group of former Mattel employees who approached the product as they would have approached any new toy prototype. They tested a wide range of compounds in varying combinations, settling eventually on silicone with a thin polyurethane film covering for the basic model. They also contrived several variants to accommodate different types of surgery (radical or modified radical mastectomies), different bra sizes, and different price points (ending up with a range that ran from $104 to $140).

Handler was a marketing genius. She knew herself to be Nearly Me's greatest asset, but since she could not be everywhere at once, she trained others to be like her and to serve as effective stand-ins. She coined the (extremely infelicitous) term "mastectomee" to designate the woman for whom her breast forms were designed. Not only did she target this woman as her customer, she also conscripted her into the Nearly Me marketing vanguard. High-end department stores—in the early years, the exclusive purveyors of Handler's products—were asked to employ selected "mastectomees" as experienced fitters. The presence of sales personnel who were themselves converts to the new products instantly transformed the hitherto miserable experience of shopping for prostheses. Gone was the dread most women felt approaching saleswomen who were uninformed and often unkind. Suddenly there was an intimacy that bonded shopper to shop assistant; the two became sympathetic co-conspirators at a time when breast cancer was still very much a secret and the loss of a breast a source of great shame.

This inspired pairing generated many satisfied customers, and Handler received letters from women who were genuinely delighted with her products. These unsolicited testimonials remind us of the lifelong consequences of radical mastectomies. Handler herself said that the pain from hers never abated. Yet she opted to have her second breast removed prophylactically in 1992 at the age of seventy-six, three years after discovering preinvasive cancer in a routine checkup.

Perhaps less surprisingly, she disapproved of breast implants, citing infections, scarring, and leaking silicone. Implant surgery represented the competition, incorporating a new type of prosthetic device designed to re-create a breast from the inside. The kind of science—and budget—required to develop implants that would not be rejected by (or toxic to) the body far outstripped

101

Handler's R&D capacity. She was, after all, a veteran of the toy industry, not a research chemist; she knew she had reached the end of the line. How she would feel about today's breast reconstruction techniques, which have nearly done away with manufactured products altogether, relying instead on "parts" supplied by the patient herself, is hard to know.

There is no question that sales of breast forms have suffered with the rise in popularity of both surgical implants and autogenous breast reconstruction following mastectomy. The pads have definitely been relegated to second-class status in the dazzling new world of bionic breasts, especially now that federal legislation requires health insurers to pay for them. And yet, despite the obvious appeal of the newer options, the choice of a nonsurgical response to the loss of a breast remains as valid as ever. Given the serious potential risks of all types of surgical breast reconstructions and the many women for whom further surgery is not an option, external forms still deserve a hearing.

The strengths and weaknesses of external prostheses have in fact never been properly assessed. According to Irene R. Healey, a prosthesis designer, virtually no serious evidence-based evaluation has been undertaken of the performance, safety, or comfort of external prostheses. Proper research, Healey argued, would certainly enhance the development of what is both a noninvasive and cost-effective approach to the care of the post-mastectomy patient.[53] With as many as 50,000 newly diagnosed women still opting for simple or modified mastectomies every year, surely the true costs and benefits of all postsurgical options need to be fully and fairly represented.

ཚེ ཚེ ཚེ

Mastectomies fell to their lowest rate ever around the time this article was written. Since then, the trend has been unmistakably upwards. This is true for women of all ages but especially for women under 50. More women are now choosing to have breast reconstruction. And, in the hope of reducing their future risk of disease, more are opting to have both breasts removed, the healthy one and the diseased. The use of this procedure (called a contralateral prophylactic mastectomy) has more than doubled in recent years.

6 ❦
Body Language

Over the past two decades, books on breast cancer have multiplied, filling shelves in the bookshops that are now devoted exclusively to women's illnesses. Twenty years ago, when these shelves were virtually empty, women were dying at almost the same high rates as those prevailing today, but drawing attention to this grim statistic was unthinkable. For women diagnosed before the mid-Seventies, making a fuss was literally more than their lives were worth.

The appearance of the first generation of cancer memoirs must be seen in the context of this conspiracy of silence. The early chronicles were really acts of daring. By speaking out, women proved that they could actually survive the treatment ordeal and, rather than agreeing to disappear into the shadowy world of the disfigured, could instead return to tell their tales, animated by a sense of

This review appeared in *The Nation*, December 1996.

purpose. Even more shocking, they demonstrated that women could involve themselves in decisions about their own course of treatment. This was revolutionary.

The experience of breast cancer was carried into public view by women who were already established writers. Rose Kushner (*Breast Cancer: A Personal History and Investigative Report*, 1975) was a *Washington Post* science writer; Betty Rollin (*First, You Cry*, 1976) an NBC correspondent; Rosamond Campion (*The Invisible Worm*, 1972) a fiction editor at *Seventeen*; and Audre Lorde (*The Cancer Journals*, 1980) a well-known poet.

These writers charted the passage from one mode of treatment to the next, documenting the complexities of their emotional journey in as much detail as they gave to their account of physical therapies. What made their narratives so compelling was not just their graphic descriptions of physical trauma but their rendering of the change of consciousness that accompanied their journey through the maze of treatment. They found entrenched medical practices that had remained unchallenged — and unproven — for more than half a century, in a world where informed consent did not exist and surgical high priests could still lay down the law. As one surgeon wrote: "In regard to tumors...lynch law is by far the better procedure than 'due process.'"

Brought face to face with the contradictions and evasions of the medical profession, these pioneers chose to become difficult patients, challenging the rationale for an approach to treatment that seemed woefully out of touch. It was still common in the Seventies, for example, to carry out a breast biopsy on a woman while she was unconscious on the operating table and then to proceed directly to a radical mastectomy if the tests found a malignancy—without conferring with her at all. To enter this inner sanctum and question the sacred rites of surgery was a call to arms.

Here was an opportunity to end the code of silence by taking that most intimate of literary genres, the diary, and opening it up. The writers transformed personal stories into public platforms. Brandishing their own case histories as cautionary tales, they helped to introduce radical changes in both the perception and management of the disease. Today's widespread use of breast-conserving surgery, for example, is at least partially attributable to the refusal by some of these writers—and, in increasing numbers, their readers—to undergo radical mastectomies.

Twenty years later, the number of breast cancer

journals has grown tremendously. These newer books are a constant reminder of the persistence of the disease and its deadliness. They also document the astonishing variations in the path it takes and its toll on women's emotional and physical lives. But, moving though they invariably are, these new chroniclers are a different breed from their predecessors. In the first generation, it was established writers who carried the disease into print; in the second, it is more often the disease that carries the writers. Musa Mayer (*Examining Myself: One Woman's Story of Breast Cancer Treatment and Recovery*, 1993) was a community mental health counselor; Rosalind MacPhee (*Picasso's Woman: A Breast Cancer Story*, 1996) was a paramedic. Juliet Wittman, whose *A Century of Breast Cancer Journal Petals* was nominated for the National Book Award in 1993, was, more typically for the genre, a writer and teacher.

Whereas the earlier cancer journals were often memoirs with a mission, front-line dispatches, the newer books turn away from this larger engagement with the disease to opt instead for a more idiosyncratic and/or introspective approach. Titles mirror the change, shifting from the exigent *"First Do No Harm…": A Dying Woman's Battle Against the Physicians and Drug Companies Who Misled Her*

About the Hazards of the Pill (1976) to the positively laid-back *Breast Cancer? Let Me Check My Schedule!* almost twenty years later.

The spread of these diaries owes a great deal to changes in the status of the disease itself, both medical and social. Thanks to earlier detection and intervention, breast cancer has now become more of a chronic condition than a life-threatening emergency; there are almost two million women in the United States today who are survivors. Thanks also to the gradual widening of media coverage, first by women's magazines and then by national newspapers, the disease has become domesticated, incorporated openly into daily routines and conversations. It has gone public.

By now, the impact of the disease on a woman's body, on her personal and family relationships, on her expectations of life, are all well known. The motivation for so many of the earlier writers—the need to bear witness, to enlighten an otherwise ignorant public—has disappeared. What, then, explains the proliferation of these books?

For a start, every generation is characterized by its own pattern of disease treatment; high-dose chemotherapy and bone marrow transplants, for example, were not features of the cancer diaries of the Seventies. But more significant, breast cancer diaries have been caught up in the larger trend toward the public observance of private trauma. Candid personal exposés have never had such high literary value. First-person accounts of every disease and disorder from back pain to manic depression find sympathetic readers. Most of these stories are intimate: Treatment failures or their uncertain outcomes are interpreted through the narrow prism of individual personality rather than viewed more dispassionately through a broader historical lens.

Creatures of the Nineties, these tales are more "a thousand points of light" than a concentrated beam aimed at the inadequacies or failures of the health care system. They reflect our contemporary view of suffering, which sees the solutions to personal afflictions (like alcoholism and sexual abuse) as the responsibility of the individual rather than society. The journey chronicled by many of the newer cancer diaries—from discovery through denial to enlightened acceptance—sends the message that, given the right attitude, women can take charge and overcome breast cancer. By implication, those who fail (i.e., those who *die* or simply those for whom the experience is not in some way uplifting) demonstrate a lack of moral courage, perseverance, and general grasp of all those virtues associated with a "go ahead" attitude.

With this tendency to be bullish if not down-right Pollyanna-ish about breast cancer, it is not surprising to find that most of the diaries published in the past ten years have upbeat endings. Take Rosalind MacPhee: "Life was full of endless possibilities," she writes at the end of *Picasso's Woman*, "and I was eager to live as fully as I could for the rest of the sweet life that was given to me. Because now I was not dying of cancer—I was living with it." This is surely what most readers want to see. The newly diagnosed patient (in a specialized reading market that grows by 185,000 *every year**) desperately needs proof that survival is possible. The more the better.

But the depressing truth is that breast cancer continues to outsmart medical science, behaving insidiously and unpredictably. When breast cancer is diagnosed after it has spread to surrounding tissue, one in four women die of the disease within five years—and the other three will never be out of the woods. For those with many other kinds of cancer, arrival at the five-year benchmark triggers a final rite of passage, this time back into the world of the well, where they are welcomed as "cured"

---

* In 2013, the expected incidence of breast cancer rose to 232,340.

and their cancers forgiven. But women with breast cancer are not so lucky. Their death rates remain elevated for twenty-five to thirty years after the original diagnosis. Breast cancer remains a killer, however unpopular it may be to say so.

One memoir, Christina Middlebrook's *Seeing the Crab*, meets this head on—its subtitle is *A Memoir of Dying*. A Jungian analyst diagnosed at forty-nine with a cancer that had already spread to her spine, Middlebrook takes up her story well past the point most other diaries end; she knows she is going to die, sooner rather than later. She knows that for her, treatment will be palliative, not curative. Nonetheless, she is able to give a wonderfully written and often humorous account of her passage through desperate remedies. The catalogue of side effects is staggering. She loses her appetite, her ability to swallow, her fingernails, her capacity to walk unaided, to urinate, to defecate. She makes us realize how various are the tasks of the body that not only constitute our notion of health but also contribute to our definition of self. Middlebrook loses not just head hair but eyelashes and underarm and pubic hair as well. With them go all the bodily odors by which she implicitly recognizes her animal existence. One of the pleasures of her recovery from treatment is the reappearance of these odors and the trips to the dry cleaners that they occasion.

Every step of the way, Middlebrook challenges the bromides, evasions, and denials of others that express their dreadful discomfort with her situation. She chooses to take an active interest in the prospect of her own death, to become what she calls a "dier" and accept that her "only ally is surrender." Cutting through the self-destructive advice served up by avatars of "New Age tyranny," she rejects their suggestion that "if I have cancer I must have 'needed' it in order to resolve some previous life issue that lies rotting beneath the surface of my life." (Many chroniclers of cancer argue that the emergence of disease is an expression of a failure to reconcile emotional conflicts. Even Gloria Steinhem, whose *Ms.* Magazine has done so much to open up the discussion of breast cancer, treated her own bout with the disease more as a welcome corrective to her denial of aging than the straightforward invasion of a potentially lethal malignancy.)

Willingness to accept responsibility for a life-threatening illness can double the burden on the newly diagnosed patient. If she feels she has brought the disease upon herself then it becomes her responsibility to provide a cure. Middlebrook

113

doesn't buy it:

The implication that one's cancerous tumor is indicative of failure offends me down to my toes. The idea that death comes to those who deserve it is a cruel jibe by the currently healthy. Giving up life is terrible.... Nevertheless, we all die. To insist that one will not die because of a superior lifestyle or a favored position in the eye of God seems unconscionably arrogant.

For her the response is less judgmental—and more thoughtful. Woven into a gruesome medical saga are speculations on the use of metaphor as an aid to comprehension; whether, for example, images of war and the companionship of an imagined soldier enrich or distort her expectations of dying or whether, ultimately, any metaphors of war, cancer, or death compromise their reality. These meditations remind us that we are witnessing a battle between a mind that is fully alive, alert to the powers, pleasures, and betrayals of language, and a body that is determined to destroy it. What is so impressive about Middlebrook's diary is that while we are under its spell, we believe this to be a contest of equals.

By its very eccentricity, *Seeing the Crab* demonstrates the increasing diversity of the breast cancer literature now available. The earlier books, with no informed readership and no established genre to guide them, opened up all fronts at once; they were diary survival guide, exposé, and polemic rolled into one. Now that breast cancer has gained a foothold in the publishing world, these concerns can be disentangled from one another. Books can carve out and develop specialized areas of interest. Personal journeys are no longer needed to serve as a bridge to the wider issues involved because these can be taken up in complementary volumes of their own.

And right on cue comes the publication of the first full-length discussion of the politics of breast cancer. Written by a medical journalist with her own history of the disease, Roberta Altman's *Waking Up/Fighting Back: The Politics of Breast Cancer* provides excellent coverage of virtually all the social and political controversies that surround contemporary diagnosis and treatment, including disputes about the treatments Middlebrook endured and debates about mammography guidelines, the use of tamoxifen and high-dose chemotherapy, genetic counseling, silicone breast implants, and environmental hazards. Equally valuable parts of the book document the rise of breast cancer activism associated with each of these contentious areas in a way that will encourage many of the millions of breast cancer survivors (diarists and non-diarists alike) to participate more in the campaigns to conquer the disease, once and for all.

☙☙☙

Seventeen years later, in 2013, it's safe to say that millions of breast cancer survivors have indeed participated in breast cancer campaigns. Whether they have contributed much to conquering the disease is a different story, one taken up in the remaining essays of this book. But it's certainly true that writing about breast cancer has undergone something of a revolution, the product of changes in both the transformation of publishing and in the cultural standing of the disease.

Traditional publishers no longer accept books documenting personal encounters with disease. But women are still churning them out. There is, in fact, a veritable tsunami of journals and diaries online, as well as a healthy stream of self-published accounts offline. On the Web, women of almost every age, with every kind of breast cancer, at every stage, post regular updates on their journeys through treatment, giving often fine-grained

116

accounts of their medical ordeals and reporting exchanges with doctors and nurses, family and friends, work colleagues and health insurance companies. Unlike their predecessors, the new journals follow the experience of breast cancer in real time, so that readers become companions, caught up in the drama of an ongoing and often urgent narrative with no certain outcome.

Online media have bred a tolerance for the kind of indeterminacy that traditional books have typically discouraged. The open-endedness of the new formats can approximate the lived experience of breast cancer much more effectively than can traditional narratives. Facebook and blog posts are usually unprocessed first responses to recent events, raw and immediate. More traditional books, like those discussed above, are typically written retrospectively, when their authors have had a chance to think back on their experience and to apply more critical judgment to what they have been through from the perspective of where they are at the time of writing.

Online, there is no need for writers to adhere to narrative conventions, shaping their stories with a view to what will follow—or polishing their prose. It is all much more informal and im- promptu. With readers encouraged to respond by posting comments, tweeting, and chatting, the back-and-forth can come close to conversational exchanges. The breast cancer diarist has become a team player; so too have all of her readers. Open and free access grants them a path to companionship, an escape from the isolation of the past.

Judging by the proliferation of these websites and the number of visitors they attract, the loss of whatever literary pleasures were to be had from published books in the genre seems to have been more than outweighed by the blogger's usefulness to a much wider readership than the books could ever hope for.

The heightened visibility of these blogs has raised hackles in some quarters. Opinion pieces by Bill Keller in the *New York Times* and by his wife Emma Keller in the Guardian ask whether there might be such a thing as Too Much Information and question the ethics of dying in such a public forum. Both Kellers take issue, specifically, with the blog and tweets of Lisa Bonchek Adams, a 37-year old woman whose posts describe in great detail every aspect of treatment for—and life with—metastatic disease. The Kellers' columns reveal not just a lack of understanding about the nature of breast cancer but a serious misreading of Bonchek Adams' own approach to it.[54] Their disapproval may in reality simply mask discomfort, with both the shadow of death hovering over all these blogs and with the public outing of a disease that once appeared to be well-behaved because it was silently endured out of sight and represented in print by women who called themselves survivors. Writers like Bonchek Adams shatter these comforting fictions.

Blogs may have captured the media's attention but books have not gone out of fashion altogether. Today, however, they are more likely to focus on cultural rather than medical ramifications of the disease. A new alliance has emerged between breast cancer and corporate America, in the form of national charities and foundations. This has attracted a new kind of attention, the result of large-scale fund-raising events produced with the help of massive public relations campaigns. As part of their promotional drives, charity directors have often been re-packaged (and financially rewarded) as celebrities, putting their personal stamp on the organizations they run.

Some of these new leaders behave more like corporate executives than directors of traditional nonprofits. And like the CEOs of private companies, they too have taken up their pens, putting their celebrity to work on behalf of the cause, becoming cultural icons in the process. Nancy

Brinker, CEO of Susan G. Komen for the Cure, has written three books, all versions of the same story. The multiple re-telling of the origins of the Komen legend — growing out of a promise made to a sister dying from breast cancer in 1980 — has become a kind of corporate foundation myth.

When Komen withdrew funding from Planned Parenthood in 2012, it generated a virtual media frenzy. The architect of the policy, Karen Handel, who quickly resigned from her position as senior vice president, rushed into print in Komen's defense, with a book called *Planned Bullyhood: The Truth Behind the Headlines About the Planned Parenthood Funding Battle with Susan G. Komen for the Cure* (2012).

There are countervailing voices, too, that speak out against the excesses of pink ribbon enthusiasms and document their damaging effects, such as Gayle Sulik's *Pink Ribbon Blues: How Breast Cancer Culture Undermines Women's Health* (2012). Columns representing all shades of opinion on this and other related controversies have become common. They often are written by men. And many of the newer writers have no personal history of the disease at all.

What this contest of issues and ideologies points to is the coming of age of breast cancer as a social issue of concern to a national audience, on a par with issues like abortion and gay marriage. Now everyone can have an opinion; insider knowledge is no longer required. This is a far cry from the days of the earliest breast cancer chroniclers. Closeted with their illness, often with little hope of surviving, they had no larger sisterhood to turn to, no organized support to encourage them and no disinterested audience to validate them.[55] What they did have was unusual courage and a belief in the therapeutic power of language.

7❦
The Last Word: Obituaries

My mother grew up believing that women never died. After all, she reasoned, she never saw an obituary of a woman in a newspaper. Men, on the other hand, lived heroic lives in the public arena and were cruelly cut down by old age, disease, and occasionally, by other men.

At their death, men's lives, like their bodies, were tidied up for eternity. Like epitaphs cut into tombstones, they were built to last, to be the Last Word. Distilling the messy raw material of life into a streamlined story, obituaries reflected prevailing ideas of the virtuous public life. Airbrushed out of the picture were all the complicating factors of character, temperament, family and personal connections, all those features that help to animate a life story. So assiduously did obituaries strip away all flesh-and-blood details, in fact, that

This article appeared first in *Sojourner:The Women's Forum*, March 1998.

their publication often marked a kind of second death, leaving the reader with a lifeless portrait of sanctified achievement, purified of all personal entanglements.

This traditional emphasis on male self-mastery and the obituary's uninflected roll call of life events made it very hard to accommodate women; they lived much of the time in a domestic world that obituaries never acknowledged. Women themselves had no expectation of any such recognition. "Anonymity runs in their blood," wrote Virginia Woolf in the 1920s. "The desire to be veiled still possesses them. They are not even now as concerned about the health of their fame as men are, and speaking generally, will pass a tombstone or a signpost without feeling an irresistible desire to cut their names on it."[56]

Their lives, in any case, were not easily adapted to the requirements of the obituary format. They did not move forward in an unbroken line of worldly accomplishments but followed their own, less linear paths. These often strayed off the page altogether, looping in and out of view at unpredictable intervals. With apparent disregard for the tyrannies of chronology, women's lives mixed the "productive" with the "reproductive" in combinations that defied easy categorizing. To attempt to condense them into a simple summing up would inevitably compromise the obituary's simplified story line.

The poor fit between the life and the life story helps to explain both the historic delay in reporting the deaths of women and the curious denaturing of those women's lives once they were covered, reconfigured as they often were to fit the male model. Even now, some obituaries still give off a whiff of the gentleman's club. But if we don't expect to see many women's portraits lining the walls of these establishments, we do at least recognize that membership in the club has now been extended to them.

The admission of women to obituary columns has, like the admission of women everywhere else, altered the nature of the beast. Traditionally, obituaries have been slow to reveal the cause of death. The perennial use of the euphemism "after a long illness bravely borne" made it possible to keep the intimacy and the messiness of death at arm's length. It preserved the idea of dying as a controlled event, with its own rules of decorum. A good death ran parallel to a good life; both required manly and orderly behavior. For men in particular, any disclosure of actual suffering would violate the formality of the occasion, undermining the illusion

of a dying man presiding over his death in much
the same way he had presided over his life. Any
show of emotional distress or pain would also be
out of step with the more upbeat portrayal of the
life that the obituary enters into the record. And
it is the life that matters. Death may provide the
occasion, but it is not the obituary's true subject.
After passing on the bare mortal facts, an obituary
quickly sets them aside, retreating at once to the
much safer ground of biography.

Women's obituaries have forged a closer connection between life and death. As caregivers of
the sick and dying, women are presumed to be
familiar with physical ailments and less likely to be
squeamish about the body. There is an expectation that their greater intimacy with the process
of birth, the beginning of life, somehow bestows
on them an easier acceptance of its end as well.
Or maybe their presumed familiarity with the so-
called life forces is just a projection of the male
writer, who hopes to insulate himself from his
own inevitable end by recasting death as a female
adornment. Whatever the reasons, whether these
responses are simply unexamined prejudices or
legitimate observations, they have made a mention
of dying more acceptable in women's obituaries.

This hasn't come upon us all at once but reflects

incremental changes over a long period of time. The gradual disclosure of breast cancer in death notices over the past century reveals the slow shift toward a more open accommodation of disease and death. It also offers, in miniature, a summary history of the changes in cultural awareness that have taken place over the last half century.

For the evidence of this progression, we are indebted to those women whose lives were just too exceptional to exclude from the newspaper. As it turns out, it is not just their lives that have taught us something of value; it is also their deaths. And though probably only one of these women would have considered herself a cancer activist, the end-of-life experiences of all of them have nonetheless enlarged our understanding of the social history of the disease.[57]

Our general awareness of breast cancer is of relatively recent origin. What we know of its nine-teenth-century impact comes from late twentieth-century scholarship. No newspapers, for example, reported on the death in 1892 of Alice James, diarist and smart sister of William and Henry. Yet we know from a recent biography that she was completely aware of her own breast cancer. She had discovered a lump herself and understood that her refusal of treatment would hasten what she called

her "mortuary moment."
   The first public discussion of cancer occurred

ALICE JAMES

128

about twenty years after James's death, in an article published in the *Ladies' Home Journal* in 1913. Early campaigns to increase awareness of the "dread disease" did not distinguish between cancers at different sites in the body. This made it much more sinister; cancer could strike at random anywhere—and kill. With this kind of power, it's not surprising that the disease became demonized. So dangerous was the Hydra-headed monster that even referring to it by name could attract the "evil eye"; any approach had to be veiled behind the "c-word."

The gradual isolation of breast cancer as a separate disease in its own right has obviously had an enormous impact on every aspect of the illness, from basic research at one extreme to the everyday consciousness of women at the other. But even before it acquired independent standing, there was already a tendency to view cancer as a woman's disease. Promoted by education campaigns in the 1920s and 1930s, widely circulated slogans claimed that "more women die of cancer than do men" or that "cancer afflicts women in a very much larger proportion than it does men."[58] This early depiction of cancer as a disease of women (contrasting with heart disease as a male affliction) may help to explain why references to it, even if still quite rare,

129

do begin to appear in women's obituaries before the Second World War.

One of these exceptional references appeared in the obituary of Charlotte Perkins Gilman, the social reformer and writer (*The Yellow Wallpaper*, *Herland*). Diagnosed with breast cancer in 1932, Gilman refused to undergo a mastectomy and determined to kill herself when her illness became unbearable. Three years later, she carried out her plan. Newspapers reporting her death made great play of the fact that she had taken her own life and quoted liberally from her suicide note. "Public opinion," she had written, "is changing on this subject. The time is approaching when we shall consider it abhorrent to our civilization to allow a human being to lie in prolonged agony which we should mercifully end in any other creature.... Believing this choice to be of social service in promoting wiser views on this question, I have preferred chloroform to cancer."

Gilman's courage (like her obituary) is focused on her death, not on her disease. Cancer was still untouchable as a subject. As long as breast cancer remained invisible inside the larger, formless terror, it could not become an adversary in the public imagination. Gilman, who had fought so hard for the recognition of a distinctly feminist

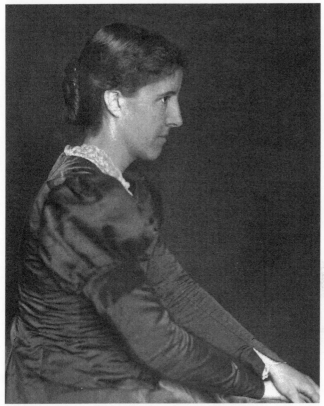

CHARLOTTE PERKINS GILMAN

consciousness, could not bring her radical perspective to bear on her own illness. She could defy

131

the conventions of dying but not the conventional response to her disease. In the absence of a tangible target for her to address, resignation must have seemed a rational response and suicide a final bid for control of one's own suffering and death.

When Rachel Carson, the author of *Silent Spring*, died from breast cancer, the *New York Times* reported that she "had had cancer for some years," adding, in what was still an exception for the paper, the "she had been aware of her illness." This was well before doctors began to deal candidly with cancer patients, openly discussing their diagnosis and treatment with them. Surely it was Carson's own pioneering work raising our consciousness of the links between cancer and chemical pesticides that made this revelation both a pertinent and a respectful gesture. Even so, the newspaper still could not print the word "breast."

A year after Carson's death, the National Cancer Institute, for the first time, listed breast cancer as a separate entry in its annual tally of deaths. By the 1970s, the disease was well out of the closet and into the realm of public debate. Yet newspapers remained reluctant to name it. Although it had been easy for women to reveal publicly that they were living with the disease (since the early days of Betty Ford and Happy Rockefeller in the

1970s), it remained much harder for obituaries to confirm that they were still dying from it. Women, in other words, could "have" breast cancer but were still deemed to die of the more undifferentiated disease "cancer."

This was the fate of Jacqueline Susann, author of *Valley of the Dolls*, who died in 1974 aged fifty-three. Her obituary played up her long-term survival after diagnosis, emphasizing breast cancer as a chronic disease rather than as a killer. Susann "died of cancer" but she had had "surgery for breast cancer in 1962...and 10 years later began cobalt radiation treatments and chemotherapy when cancer was found in other areas."[59] This detailing of treatment over a period of years marked a new departure in reporting. The date of a woman's mastectomy was now included to serve as a marker for the onset of her protracted battle with the disease, demonstrating that breast cancer was no stealth killer; if death was predictable at least it behaved in an orderly—read "ladylike"—manner. This is, of course, highly misleading. But even in its attenuated form, no parallel description of the course of a man's illness is anywhere to be found in the 1970s. No man died of prostate cancer: prostatectomies had absolutely not entered the public discourse.

133

Almost twenty years after Susann's death, when the poet Audre Lorde, one of the most vocal and eloquent of breast cancer activists, herself died of the disease, the *New York Times* attributed her death to liver cancer rather than to breast cancer that had metastasized to her liver. This prolonged reticence must hark back to the days when obits drew a veil over domestic life and when men, acting as heads of households, kept the home shrouded in secrecy.

Perhaps the death of Rose Kushner in 1990 prompted the first use of the words "breast cancer" in the boldface heading of an obituary. This would be entirely appropriate. Breast cancer had, after all, consumed the final decades of the life of Rose Kushner as well as causing her death.[60] The publication of her obituary may mark the first formal recognition of breast cancer activism as a calling.

By the early 1990s, after the disease had become a regular feature of virtually every other newspaper column (news, science, personal health, society, even fashion), obituary editors finally took the plunge and made regular up-front disclosures of death from breast cancer (as happened at the death of May Sarton in 1995). And mastectomies now enter the public domain; they even crop up occasionally in men's obituaries. The *New York Times* write-up of the screenwriter Robert Shaw told the story of his plans for a soap opera character on *Search for Tomorrow*. He wrote that he had planned "one of the most tried-and-true plot devices in serials; a mastectomy." The long-serving actress who would undergo the surgery responded that "the mastectomy will fascinate my viewers because it will be my third."

Now that breast cancer has become almost a commonplace in obituary columns, we can see much more clearly how the disease cuts down women in their prime (only two of the six women I've mentioned—Charlotte Perkins Gilman and May Sarton—actually made it to old age). Sadly, any review of death notices today will turn up a non-negligible number of women in their forties and fifties, an age group for which breast cancer is the leading cause of death.

With the death of Kathy Acker at age fifty-three in December 1997, the battle to fight the disease has finally become integrated with the life story itself. Most obituaries of this American performance artist, biker girl, and novelist (*Blood and Guts in High School*) include some description of her final illness. The British *Guardian* devoted a considerable portion of its obituary to a retelling

135

of Acker's reaction to her diagnosis (she had chosen to undergo a double mastectomy but refused chemotherapy).

> Okay, so I have always believed the men in the white coats had all the answers.But they didn't. It was like they had taken all the meaning from my body. I thought. I will not die a meaningless death. I will find out the answers. I will make myself well or at least I will die in control of my body.

In a series of articles written for the British press during the year before she died, Acker documented her experience of breast cancer and her eventual rejection of conventional treatment. She believed that if she "remained in the hands of conventional medicine" she "would soon be dead, rather than diseased, meat." So her "search for a way to defeat cancer now became a search for life and death that were meaningful." This insistence on finding her own way through her ordeal, defining her own experience of disease, reflects the same defiance of orthodoxy that marks most of her other work. And even though her struggle was ultimately unsuccessful, her relentless engagement with the meaning of her illness (and with the relation of her beliefs to her body) forced itself into her obituaries. There it challenged the traditional view of death as just a final curtain or the abrupt interruption of a life which paid it no attention. Acker brings the life *with* and the death *from* breast cancer into a kind of alignment that obituaries have traditionally withheld from their readers.

KATHY ACKER
PHOTO COURTESY OF MARCUS LEATHERDALE

Acker's voice is one of the more recent in a long succession of outspoken women. Accustomed to lives as public figures while they were in good health, the women mentioned here had already proved themselves capable of challenging whatever sexist barriers got in their way. So it is not surprising to find them rejecting recommended treatments (like Gilman and Acker) or sharing their experience of breast cancer (like Lorde and Acker). Rachel Carson chose to keep her illness private. She feared that public exposure of her own breast cancer would compromise the reception of *Silent Spring*, which took an extremely controversial position linking the long-term use of man-made chemicals to cancer. As she wrote to a friend, "I have no wish to read of my ailments in literary gossip columns. Too much comfort to the chemical companies."[61] Jaqueline Susann did not publicly discuss her treatment either but she made her views plain enough in her fiction; one of her characters in *Valley of the Dolls* chooses to kill herself rather than undergo a mastectomy.

Each of the women caught up in this struggle has expressed an attitude toward the sacrifice of her own life that has, bit by bit, moved us forward, toward a more uncompromising and unsentimental view of disease. It has taken almost a century for obituaries to acknowledge publicly that women do die, that cancer kills many of them, that breast cancer is a chronic disease of its own, of unknown origins and uncontrollable outcomes, and that the treatments for it that we have been offered for decades are inadequate.

Of course, we knew many of these things before we saw them in print, but their appearance on the page has liberated them from the general hypocrisy that colors most obituaries and renders their subjects so lifeless. Seeing is believing. So, in a sense, the penetration of breast cancer into obituary columns might have a liberating effect on the form itself, as more obit writers, enlightened by their coverage of women, come to question the long-held assumptions that once governed our views of the exemplary life and death. These turn out, like our understanding of the disease itself, not to be written in stone after all.

༜༜༜

Fifteen years after this article was written, the representation of breast cancer has, indeed, changed quite a bit. Perhaps nothing better illustrates the

altered landscape than the obituary of the activist Barbara Brenner who died in May 2013. For
fifteen years, Barbara served as the   first Executive Director of Breast Cancer Action. BCA was
the first organization to recognize the disease as a
political issue and the first to refuse funding from

BARBARA BRENNER
PHOTO COURTESY OF DAVID TOERGE

corporations that might profit from or contribute to cancer. Barbara retired from BCA in 2010. Her obituary in the *New York Times* identifies her not as a victim of breast cancer—she did not die of the disease, although she had endured two bouts with it—but as a "breast cancer iconoclast" who saw the disease as a problem for society as much as an affliction to be suffered individually.[62] Impatient for change, she fearlessly—and tirelessly—questioned the prevailing assumptions and practices governing our response to the disease, starting with the language we use to describe it. As her obituary relates, she stood up at a medical conference and "scolded a researcher who had described patients as failing treatment. Patients do not fail treatments, she told him—treatments fail patients."

With the same bedrock commitment to truth-telling, Brenner took on all the players in the breast cancer arena, most prominently perhaps, the "pinkwashers" (as she was the first to call them), the corporations that exploited the disease for profit. She also railed against the excessive promotion of screening mammography, a billion-dollar industry that promised more than it could deliver, and the inflated claims of drug companies involved in treatment.

As her obituary reports with a candor once

unheard of, Brenner took on other breast cancer groups as well, those that were all too eager to accommodate corporate agendas, for fear of losing sponsorship. She attacked "Susan G. Komen for the Cure for teaming up with KFC to produce pink buckets of chicken. Fried chicken, she said, promotes obesity, which is a risk factor for breast cancer." This kind of challenge put something of a dent in the image of "awareness" that drives much of Komen's advocacy work. That Breast Cancer Action's campaign—"What the Cluck?"—generated controversy points to the disease's enhanced status as a national issue, as rife with conflicts of interest and big money as any other major social concern.

The *New York Times* obit had called the activist Rose Kushner "vigorous and tenacious." Twenty years later, it described Barbara Brenner's approach as "fiery" "blunt" and "tart" and lets her speak, unapologetically, for herself: "We serve no purpose in being nice." And where Kushner, acting largely on her own, had narrowly targeted what she perceived as abuses in the surgical treatment of breast cancer with impressive results, Brenner, with Breast Cancer Action behind her, was able to cast her net more widely, setting her sights on the limitations/potential hazards of available diagnosis and treatment, the inadequacy of health care, and the shameful lack of investment in prevention.

In a final jab at shopworn obituary etiquette, Suzanne Lampert, Brenner's partner of forty years, delivers the last word: "I always told her that I would make sure her obituary said she died after a long battle with the breast cancer industry."

8 ❦
Shopping for the Cure

Millions of American women are now running, swimming, and climbing for breast cancer, raising extraordinary sums of money for charities whose workings they know almost nothing about. This odd throwback to the earliest breast cancer fundraising campaigns of the 1930s may go unnoticed because the outward appearances are so radically changed. But although spandex and sweatbands have replaced white gloves and hats, and biking has replaced baking, women are once again donating their time, energy, and money, *no questions asked*.

The Race for the Cure, one of the oldest of these athletic events, is run by the Susan G. Komen Breast Cancer Foundation, a nonprofit organization set up to fight breast cancer in 1982. In 1998, it raised over $54 million in 85 separate races. (This

This article appeared in The American Prospect, September 25–October 9, 2000.

is an aggregate figure. Komen will not say how
much of this amount went to fund-raising expenses and how much to breast cancer causes.) Joining
the bandwagon in the early 1990s, cosmetic giants
Avon and Revlon introduced sporting events of
their own. Revlon's Run/Walks for Women in New
York and Los Angeles netted $4 million in 1999
($17 million between 1993 and 1999), which the
company contributed to breast cancer charities.
The Avon Breast Cancer Crusade, which sponsors
three-day, 60-mile walks, netted $15.6 million from
its four 1999 events.

The impressive sums raised and contributed
by these corporate charities are, of course, not gifts
in the usual sense (that is, donations out of company profits). They are the contributions made by
millions of volunteer athletes and their support-
ers, bundled together, repackaged, and released
under the corporate logo of the organizing charity. As facilitators of this transformation process,
participating companies gain for themselves an
immeasurable amount of public goodwill. And because they are dealing with unrestricted donations
from volunteers rather than investments from
shareholders, they are essentially unaccountable
for how they distribute the funds.

It is not only Komen that takes this opportunity

to obscure its expenses. Just as Komen will give out only gross numbers from its athletic events, Revlon and Avon will give out only net numbers. But it appears that the Avon Breast Cancer Crusade spends more than a third of the funds it raises in its three-day events on advertising, event expenses, and overhead. The Crusade's literature puts it this way: "The Avon 3-Days have delivered over $25 million to the breast cancer cause since 1998, representing a 60% return." At Komen, one spokesperson told me that the foundation keeps race expenses for its one-day events below 25 percent of race revenues (not counting cash and in-kind donations from corporate sponsors); others refuse to confirm that and will say only that the foundation's overall expenses amount to 9 percent of overall revenue. Revlon says its expenses for its one-day Run/Walks are about 11 percent of revenues (including the contributions of corporate sponsors).

Obviously, the three organizations' expense figures are neither clear nor comparable—given the variety of ways revenues are accounted for and differences in the nature of the events—but all would seem substantial enough to pique participants' curiosity. Oddly, they have not.

For participants what seems to count is not this kind of operational detail, but their own public involvement in the fight against the disease and their ability to make a show of their numbers. Likewise, they expect the media coverage of these events to convey the vast toll that breast cancer has taken on the lives of American women and the physical courage of those who have survived, rather than any urgent demands for new research priorities or stronger public policies. In this, the athletic events differ markedly from the political demonstrations of the breast cancer movement in the early 1990s, which the races have largely come to replace.

Ten years ago, women from community cancer projects gathered on the steps of state capitols, and, after 1991, the National Breast Cancer Coalition appeared before Congress to protest the lack of adequate funding for breast cancer research. The demonstrations drew attention to the sexual politics of the disease, proclaiming a link between the historic exclusion of women from all aspects of relevant public policy making and the historic failure of the mainstream cancer establishment to stem the rising tide of breast cancer deaths. To bring down the death rate, the demonstrators of the early 1990s insisted, required more than just money (although that was clearly essential); it also depended upon the active participation of

148

women themselves. Breast cancer advocacy groups run by and on behalf of women were expected to reeducate the policy makers. For instance, they wanted to get across the idea that research about treatments—research about the things that actually happen to patients—is as necessary as basic science research.

The early advocacy groups more than lived up to those expectations. Their lobbying efforts not only helped to raise annual federal spending on breast cancer research from $90 million a decade ago to $660 million in 1999; they also succeeded in involving women at almost every level of decision making that affects national breast cancer policy. To this day, the National Breast Cancer Coalition's Project LEAD offers intensive four-day science courses for advocates, to enable them to participate on funding review boards where they represent the perspective of the breast cancer patient.

Project LEAD receives generous funding from Avon. But at the same time, advocacy activities have been thoroughly upstaged by the new corporate charities. What the public and the policy makers hear about breast cancer nowadays is not a political message. Applying for-profit public relations skills (and budgets) to nonprofit operations, the corporate charities have succeeded in branding breast cancer imagery.

The new logos and slogans everywhere promote products for sale. JCPenney, one of the Komen national sponsors, offers 25 percent discount coupons to all Race for the Cure participants. Hallmark's Cards for the Cure and Goldsmith Seeds' Plant for the Cure, among many others, donate a percentage of the proceeds from sales of particular items or on a particular day to the Komen foundation. Even Charles Schwab weighed in at one point with a Commission for the Cure, contributing to Komen the commissions charged for online trades placed on Mother's Day.

The emphasis on consuming as a way of raising money—shopping for the cure—trades on the most conventional expectations of women rather than on their capacity for social action. Nonetheless, the new breast cancer events are widely seen as upsetting conventions. In striving to achieve longer distances or faster times, or, in the case of survivors, just to demonstrate their recovery from punishing cancer treatments, the athletes who participate appear to be pushing the envelope. The same metaphors and sense of deliberate provocation attach to the enterprise as a whole, as though the collective energy and determination generated by the races have constituted an aggressive challenge to the status quo.

As it has turned out, however, these breast cancer charities have followed a quite traditional model in selecting beneficiaries for their largesse. Both the American Cancer Society, the oldest and still most powerful cancer charity, and the government's National Cancer Institute spend their money largely on public education (urging people to take screening tests), support services (like driving patients to the hospital), screening procedures, and orthodox biomedical research; neither organization pays much attention to the possible links between cancer and man-made environmental toxins. The new philanthropies have had an opportunity to redress those biases and have been encouraged to do so by breast cancer activists. Alas, they have not.

Most egregiously, they have mirrored the cancer establishment's traditional reluctance to get involved in paying for proper diagnosis and treatment for women who can't afford them. Not until 1990 was federal funding finally made available, through the Centers for Disease Control (CDC), to provide breast and cervical cancer screening for low-income women ineligible for Medicaid or Medicare. And despite significant growth in that program over the past ten years, its funding in

2000 (at $167 million) is still so low that it provides screening, by the government's own estimate, for only 15 percent of eligible women. Worse yet, in the original 1990 legislation, Congress allocated no funds at all to pay for the follow-up treatment of any women diagnosed with cancer through a CDC-sponsored screening program. These women, with the help of their health care providers, were expected to seek charity care on a catch-as-catch-can basis.

Study after study has demonstrated that this doesn't work. Early detection may save middle-class lives, but the numbers are far different for women without adequate insurance. Yet Komen, Avon, and Revlon have followed the cancer establishment's slow lead—in recent years funding mammography for low-income women, but still no further treatment. Indeed, most breast cancer charities have paid generously for everything but surgery, radiation, and chemotherapy. They've covered biopsies, pain medication, transportation to and from treatment, child care—all very much needed services—but nothing that could be construed as breaking the American taboo on "socialized medicine."

There have been exceptions to this rule, both large and small. Cancer Care, a national agency with annual revenues of almost $14 million in 1999, has had funding from the New York Community Trust since the mid-1980s to pay directly for the costs of cancer treatment for New Yorkers. In 1999 about 600 patients received direct financial support from Cancer Care. At the other end of the spectrum, the Bridge Breast Center in Dallas operates with a staff of three and a total budget of $450,000, funded in part by a local affiliate of the Komen Foundation. In 1999 Bridge managed to see 310 women with a suspicious breast lump and paid for the treatment of the 42 among them who were diagnosed with a malignancy.

To date, these programs remain exceptional, though if the government starts paying for cancer treatment, there are signs that the charities may follow suit. In 1999 a bill was introduced in Congress to spend money on treatment of uninsured women diagnosed with cervical or breast cancer; the following spring, the Avon Breast Cancer Crusade announced grants of $2.5 million for clinical treatment services for "medically underserved women," including surgery, radiation, and chemotherapy. This year (2000) the Breast and Cervical Cancer Prevention and Treatment Act (H.R. 4386) passed the House, 421 to one, and should it pass the Senate, $250 million has been budgeted for the program over the next five years—perhaps 15 to 20 percent of what's needed to treat the 30,000 uninsured and underinsured women diagnosed each year. Maybe the new charities will then try to make up the difference.

But when it comes to cancer policy, they are not in the lead, and women racing for the cure would do well to reflect on what it takes to actually win.

೨೨೨

The Breast and Cervical Cancer Prevention and Treatment Act (H.R. 4386) *did* pass the Senate in October 2000 and was one of the last bills that President Clinton signed into law before leaving office. The law extended Medicaid coverage for breast cancer treatment to about 10 percent of American women, those who were uninsured or underinsured or below 250 percent of federal poverty level. The CDC collects data on the number of women screened and diagnosed but not on the number of women treated; that is left to the states.[63] In 2011, the program provided mammography screening for 334,300 women and diagnosed 5,781 breast cancers.

But a GAO Report published in 2009 reveals that the CDC program is still reaching less than half its targeted population. Restrictions on funding have limited CDC screening to about 15 percent of the women who are eligible. Some states make it much harder than others to qualify for Medicaid. Breast cancer charities have picked up some of the slack, providing free clinics and mobile vans that reach another 26 percent. But that still leaves 60 percent of eligible women out in the cold.

The Affordable Care Act of 2010 *should* increase access to breast and cervical cancer screening services for many of the same population, through expanded health insurance coverage and tax credits. The new law also requires health insurance plans to provide breast cancer screening services without cost-sharing. How these legislated improvements will work out on the ground is, however, still unknown.

9 ❦
The Tyranny of Cheerfulness: Pink Ribbons, Inc.

Twenty-one years after the launch of Breast Cancer Awareness month, October 2006 brought us pink Playtex rubber gloves, pink Goddess hair extensions, pink Hooters Girl Uniform cards, and pink bustiers auctioned off at the Crittenton Hospital Medical Center in Rochester, Michigan. It's hard to imagine a list that more succinctly captures stereotypical images of female vanity and sexist body language. Yet all these items—and thousands more just like them—are sold in the name of high-minded concern for women with breast cancer, as the companies flogging them pledge to contribute some share of the income to "the cause." Women are responding to these appeals in their millions, no questions asked, producing windfall profits for many of those on the corporate breast-cancer bandwagon.

What could explain women's wholesale capitulation to these regressive marketing ploys, which

This first appeared in *Women's Review of Books* 24/2, March–April 2007.

cast them as undiscerning shoppers and dumb down responses to a disease that kills more than 40,000 women every year? How has breast cancer advocacy of the early 1990s—including feminists' demands for increased research funding, improved treatment, and access to health care—been so effectively upstaged by corporate self-interest? Samantha King provides some thought-provoking answers to these questions. The great virtue of her book is that it interprets the success of breast cancer fund-raising not as an isolated phenomenon—a unique response to a unique disease—but rather as an expression of broader trends in contemporary philanthropy and politics. The pink-ribbon phenomenon, King says, reflects a recent marriage between new corporate giving strategies and what she calls "consumption-based citizenship." Corporations that once made ad hoc annual gifts to an eclectic mix of charities now focus on a single cause, one that resonates with their own product—and bottom—line. In a display of enlightened self-interest, companies have found ways to make philanthropy profitable. They hope their "financially sound goodwill" will strengthen customer loyalty and enhance brand recognition.

Meeting them halfway is a public newly awakened to the virtues of personal and corporate generosity and so-called ethical volunteerism, that stand in opposition to the welfare state's culture of dependency. The idea is that the focused efforts of engaged citizens, set in motion by civic-minded corporations, might one day actually outperform Big Government and its collective (read: failed) solutions to social problems.

Both trends are driven by national politics. Behind the rhetoric of "a thousand points of light" (George H. W. Bush's characterization of the pooled power of individual philanthropy) was the drive toward broad-based privatization. George W. Bush's "Armies of Compassion" initiative carries forward the same vision. The new mantras of civic participation are self-help and personal responsibility. Forget about the social safety net and public accountability. Citizenship, like charity, now begins at home.

King traces the impact of this political perspective on all aspects of breast cancer fund-raising. She concentrates on the best-known examples—the Komen Race for the Cure, the breast cancer stamp, and the Avon three-day walk. Throughout her narratives, she never loses sight of the larger picture, making connections between the enterprising spirit of the various "thons" (marathons, walkathons, triathlons, etc.) and their reinforcement of a broader market-driven ideology.

The details are fascinating. The Komen Foundation's 5K Race for the Cure, inspired by the rise of the fitness movement in the early 1980s, was first run in Dallas in 1983 with 700 participants. By 1999, it was held annually in 99 cities across the United States. By 2005, it attracted 1.4 million participants. All Race for the Cure events share certain features, including a survivor recognition ceremony, a "wellness" area, and a place for corporate sponsors to display their products. They all look the same, so that, as King suggests, the race itself has become "a familiar and reliable brand." The Komen Foundation has, in fact, been able to trademark the phrase "for the cure" to protect its competitive advantage over competing cause-marketers.

King respects the good intentions of women participating in the race and other "thons." She highlights the useful side effects of these events— the networking opportunities and the solidarity they create among women who have undertaken similar medical journeys. But she also laments what she calls the "tyranny of cheerfulness": the embrace of the disease as a milestone on the road to true happiness. Endorphins whipped up in the Komen race no doubt create a heady sense of accomplishment. But as racing metaphors displace the older "war on cancer" imagery, competition inevitably creeps into the picture. Though the dead are often memorialized—with their names and images emblazoned on the chests and banners of participating "thoners"—they emerge here as losers. A whiff of personal failure hangs over them. King, citing Barbara Ehrenreich, points to "the triumphalism of survivorhood" that "denigrates the dead and the dying, a sense in which breast cancer survivors are understood to have somehow fought harder than those who have died."

King ties this perception that survival equals success to women's general compliance with the cancer establishment. Surviving, she argues, requires women's "submission to mainstream scientific knowledge and reliance on doctors and scientists to protect them from death." Rather than responding to their cancer experience with anger or despair—with questions about unequal access to quality care, the toxicity of drugs or the uncertainties of treatment—they become well-behaved patients, and, once restored to their friends and families, well-behaved survivors. Their appearance at fund-raising events is, in King's reading, another confirmation of the wisdom of accepting the status quo. To raise difficult questions would be to break the spell that got them into the charmed circle in the first place. It would expose them once again to risk. In bowing to the prescribed protocol and spirit of the events, whether out of fear, passivity, or positive identification, women score another victory for traditional values, including those that forbid them to challenge authority.

Of course, not all American women with an interest in breast cancer have succumbed to the blandishments of cause marketing. As an example of a far different approach, King presents Breast Cancer Action (BCA), an activist organization in California that accepts no money from the pharmaceutical companies so eager to sponsor the "thons." BCA launched an ad campaign in 2002 to raise awareness about the hypocrisy of much corporate philanthropy. The ads pointed out that for companies, the public relations value of their participation in Breast Cancer Awareness month sometimes exceeded the value of their net donations. "Will your purchase make a difference?" a BCA ad asked, "Or is the company exploiting breast cancer to boost profits?" American Express, for instance, widely publicized a "Charge for the Cure" campaign, in which it promised to donate a portion of every credit card charge during the month of October. However, the portion it donated turned out to be one penny per transaction—so it took a hundred transactions to raise one dollar for breast cancer.

King explores recent corporate efforts to take their breast cancer cause-marketing global, updating previous work on the subject. Although these efforts are still in their early stages, it's clear that companies like Avon hope their philanthropic crusades will help them establish their good-faith credentials around the world as potential partners in the development of new markets. It's too soon to tell how American-designed "thons" and other charity events will play in other cultures, which have different experiences of disease (with, say, lower rates of breast cancer) or different systems of health care provision (a national health service, for example). We will need to keep watch over this.

King focuses on the corporate response to breast cancer. As a result, she unintentionally plays down the role of the government, which is significantly more important in shaping the national response to the disease than corporations or nonprofits, despite the occasional ideological challenge. King discusses government only in relation to the breast cancer stamp, which allowed the post office, for the first time, to charge more for a stamp than its face value. The additional revenues, after costs, were donated to research. The stamp proposal won 100 percent support in Congress, while providing bipartisan opportunities galore to mine the political theme of voluntary giving as an enabler of "civic participation" and a means to "personalize the relationship between citizens and the state."

Although the net revenue from the stamp exceeded all expectations, it represents just a tiny fraction of government funding for breast cancer initiatives. The stamp, which went on sale in 1998, raised almost $3.5 million by June 2005—less than one percent of the $3.5 billion allocated to the National Cancer Institute during the same period. Like the annual shower of pink products, the stamps are part of the celebrity culture of breast cancer, the surface glitter that attracts media attention. Given the prominence of these diversions and their popularity, it's important to understand where they come from and whose interests they serve. King's deft and thoughtful interpretation of the pink ribbon phenomenon is an important wake-up call. Going against the grain, she takes a clear-eyed look at a trend that often seems to outshine the disease that put it on the map.

10❦
The Breast Cancer Donor's Dilemma: Time to Revolt?

Sixty years ago, the largest national health charities in the United States dominated the philanthropic playing field and were able to carve up the fund-raising calendar year among themselves. In the days when solicitations were still face-to-face encounters or mail campaigns, each charity within this charmed circle agreed to carry out its major campaign drive within an assigned time frame. The March of Dimes kicked off the year in January, followed by the American Heart Association, which launched its own campaign on St. Valentine's Day. Easter Seals occupied the next major holiday, followed by American Cancer Society campaigns in

This first appeared on the Truthout website on 30 October 2012.

April, and so on, with Christmas Seals bringing up the rear in December.

Competing for their charitable dollars were what came to be called community chests. These were federations of often smaller charities that agreed to participate in one combined annual fund-raising drive and divide up its revenues. They were based on a practice that emerged in the First World War, when the government asked relief agencies to coordinate a collaborative fund-raising campaign. War chests aimed at direct relief soon become permanent chests addressing a variety of welfare needs. By the middle of the twentieth century, more than half of Americans were exposed to some form of federated giving.

Precursors of the United Way, such coalitions were thought to be a more cost-efficient means of conducting campaigns, minimizing overheads and other expenses. A *New York Times* article in 1969 noted that the administrative costs of community chests ranged "from 4 per cent to 10 per cent, considerably less ... than the 25 per cent to 35 per cent overhead costs of independent charity campaigns."[64] Community chests usually operated with a skeleton staff, often composed entirely of temporary volunteers in temporary offices, much like the transient and traveling infrastructure used to conduct electoral campaigns. Chests not only trimmed the demand for volunteer workers, they also limited the potential for "donor fatigue"; contributors would buy themselves immunity from further appeals, at least for another year.

The big national charities like the March of Dimes and the American Cancer Society spurned all appeals to join federated campaigns. They were reluctant to cede control of any aspect of fundraising and knew that the money they could raise on their own would outweigh whatever share of the proceeds they would receive from a collective effort.[65] Adamant about maintaining their separate identity and independence, they rejected all invitations to collaborate. If this imposed additional expenses in the form of larger, permanent staffs and more overhead, so be it. They were out to increase donations, not to increase efficiency. Cooperation was not in the cards.

For all these charities, success depended on an ever-ready supply of volunteer women willing to go door-to-door, soliciting funds for one charity after another, one year after the next. But from the early 1960s on, there were rumblings of discontent. Women began to object to the duplication of effort involved in multiple campaigns. A league of volunteer women near Madison, Wisconsin, complained that they were becoming pariahs in their own communities. When their neighbors saw them coming, they wondered, What is it this time? Charitable collection had become an embarrassment.[66]

In 1963, the year *The Feminine Mystique* was published, the Wisconsin women mounted what was deemed a "housewives' revolt." They took it upon themselves to set aside single-charity campaigns and conduct a "Combined Health Fund Drive." Their chosen beneficiaries included the American Cancer Society, the March of Dimes, and the Muscular Dystrophy Association. The big charities were not amused. In fact, all three returned the checks that had been collected on their behalf. The women were undaunted. They decided to repeat the experiment the next year, stipulating that any funds that were returned to them this time would be handed over to the University of Wisconsin for medical research. In response, the American Cancer Society decided to be more accommodating; it allowed its name to be used in the campaign on condition that fund-raisers obtain their approval in advance and provide the names and contact information for all those making donations. The other charities imposed similar conditions that allowed them to accept designated donations without losing face. In other words, no funds were rejected. The women volunteers took this as a victory.

It would be another twenty years before cancer charities figured out how to repurpose volunteer enthusiasm. In the 1980s, they discovered athletic events—walks, runs, swims—that liberated women from their door-to-door drudgery and moved them to a public venue where they could pick up the pace, extend the distance, and find sponsorship and companionship along the way.

By then, the charity landscape had radically changed. Gone, for most national players, was the commitment to a single, fixed, annual campaign. Though some charities kept their association with specific times of the year (as did the Easter Seals and Christmas Seals), most began to drift toward the state of play that prevails today, when no day in 365 is off-limits to fund-raising, and no day belongs, by custom or practice, to any one charity. The blurring of long-respected turf boundaries helped to undermine another important social belief—the idea that every disease required one, and only one, major philanthropic organization to promote its interests.

Today, such an approach strikes us as impossibly naive, now that both diseases and charities have proliferated beyond counting. The National

Cancer Institute lists well over a hundred different types of cancer, and there are nonprofit advocacy groups serving every one of them. Not surprisingly, the most commonly occurring cancers receive the most attention and the most money. Charity Navigator, for example, lists over two dozen of the largest breast cancer charities. Collectively, they raise nearly $1.7 billion a year.[67] This is not small change. It explains why competition for donors is now less intense between one disease and another than among charities serving the same disease.

It also explains why the Komen Foundation, once it had joined the ranks of the national charities, began to behave like them. Just as the big independents had once spurned community chests, Komen chose not to make common cause with other, smaller groups fighting the same battle. In 2007, it set itself apart by trademarking the slogan "for the cure," forbidding others to use it. Komen insisted that contributors to an event advertised as "Kites for a Cure," for example, might mistakenly believe they were giving to Komen. Never mind that the money might go to the same clients in the end; it would still represent an unacceptable loss of income to Komen. In seeking to protect the charity's "market share," Komen has essentially allowed the tactics of corporate self-interest to trump its philanthropic purpose. Financial success has altered its ambition. Now it may be as interested in safeguarding its own future as in promoting its original mission.

Komen's response reflects another difficulty: it is very hard to distinguish one breast cancer charity from another. Too many of these organizations are offering exactly the same thing: platitudes. "The more of us who walk, the more of us survive." "This is where the end of cancer begins." "Say yes to life." These are followed by promises of an imminent breakthrough in research or a cure just around the corner.[68]

Of course, they can't deliver on any of this. What they can deliver are endless variations on that nebulous and overworked concept, "awareness," which boils down to readily available information and advice and, possibly, access to subsidized mammography screening, genetic counseling, support groups, or a medical consultation somewhere. They are, in other words, largely pass-through operations, guiding women to resources provided by others, and paying themselves, often handsomely, for their role as middlemen or -women, no matter how hackneyed or misleading their advice. Most, for instance, still suggest that women start screening mammography at 40, despite the recommendation of the U.S. Preventive Services Task Force to start at 50, unless family or medical history dictates otherwise.[69]

There are, of course, plenty of worthwhile breast cancer nonprofits out there. Many broad-based national organizations like the YWCA and Planned Parenthood offer breast cancer services to the underserved. Charities like CancerCare provide direct, tangible benefits to patients in the form of practical and/or financial support to help pay for treatment and/or related travel or child care expenses. Other groups focus on the politics of the disease and take a more critical look at the diagnostic and treatment options that most other groups accept without demur. Finding these groups on one's own, however, can be a daunting task, especially online, where the wash of soft-focus appeals makes it difficult for donors to identify those charities that provide direct services to patients or funding for genuinely promising research. Like the frustrated volunteers in Wisconsin, today's idealists may find their zeal quickly fading in the face of so much redundancy and surfeit of pink product.

But as the Wisconsin women discovered for themselves in the 1960s, there are alternatives to consider. We could, in fact, follow their lead and resurrect the idea of federated giving campaigns. These campaigns would be stripped of their bells and whistles; they would not sponsor merchandise or events. Instead, they would focus on the end users, the organizations that carry out breast-cancer-related programs on the ground. Echoing the community chests' earlier emphasis on relief, participants would primarily be service agencies, dedicated to providing tangible help to all those at risk for the disease or affected by it in any way. Many of these groups, including those that serve minority populations, are currently too small to attract much fund-raising attention. A more inclusive coordinated campaign might help put them on a sounder financial footing. It might also create the potential for collaboration among projects that have a great deal in common.

A united fund approach would in no way interfere with the operations of existing breast cancer charities. But the availability of a more streamlined model of fund-raising, shorn of its cause marketing, its overpaid executives, and its false promises might be a godsend to committed donors who have grown disenchanted with the wasteful and often misleading tactics of pink-ribbon crusaders.

Acknowledgments

I would like to thank Sarah Flynn and Erin Clermont for their invaluable expertise — and their abiding patience. My thanks also to Sarah Fowles, Susan Franz, Suzanne Lampert, Martha Matzke, Tanya Rubbak, Gayle Sulik, Lynne Walker and Steve Walker.

My fidelity to these issues over twenty years owes a great deal to the example set by the late Barbara Brenner. Her audacity, nose for hypocrisy, and passion for truth-telling set the bar high for the rest of us toiling in these fields.

Notes

INTRODUCTION
1   It would, in fact, take another twenty years before our concerns rose to prominence on the front page of the *New York Times*. See Tara Parker-Pope, THE CANCER DIVIDE: "Tackling a Racial Gap in Breast Cancer Survival," 20 December 2013.

1 "MY SOUL IS AMONG LIONS"
2   The best known personal accounts of breast cancer from the 1970s are Rosamond Campion, *The Invisible Worm* (1972); Rose Kushner, *Breast Cancer: A Personal History and Investigative Report* (1975); and Betty Rollin, *First You Cry* (1976). For a review of the rise of breast cancer narratives, see "Body Language," chap. 6 in this book.

3   Although "survivor" memoirs predominate, there are exceptions. One of the earliest is *Cancer in Two Voices* (1991) written by Barbara Rosenblum and Sandra Butler. It reproduces the parallel journal entries of two lesbians, one dying of breast cancer and the other her partner, documenting their perspectives over the course of Rosenblum's illness until her death in 1988.

4   This is a typewritten manuscript of about 7,000 words in the Katharine Coman Papers, Wellesley

College Archives. Unless otherwise noted, all quotations refer to this document.

5 Bates began writing poetry when she was very young. A poem she published in the *Atlantic Monthly* when she was still in college caught the eye of Henry Wadsworth Longfellow. According to Dorothy Burgess, Bates's niece and biographer, when the Wellesley literary club visited the poet at his house in Cambridge, he complimented her on it (*Dream and Deed* [Norman: University of Oklahoma Press, 1952], 42). Bates wrote "America the Beautiful" after an expedition to the summit of Pikes Peak in Colorado. The poem was first published on 4 July 1895 in *The Congregationalist Magazine* and sparked a national response that included contests to supply a musical setting for the poem and efforts (unsuccessful) to adopt the poem as a national anthem.

6 For biographical information on Coman, see Allen F Davis, "Katharine Coman," in *Notable American Women, 1607–1950*, ed. Edward T James, Janet Wilson James, and Paul S Boyer (Cambridge: Harvard University Press, 1971), vol. 1, 365–67; and Gerald F Vaughn, "Katharine Coman: America's First Woman Institutional Economist and a Champion of Education for Citizenship," *Journal of Economic Issues* 38 (2004): 989–95. Judith Schwartz's "Yellow Clover: Katharine Lee Bates and Katharine Coman" is the only article I have found that focuses on the personal relationship between Bates and Coman, *Frontiers* 4/1 (1979): 59–67.

7 I have found no earlier American examples. However,

the English novelist Fanny Burney, best known for her novel *Evelina*, published a famous account of her breast cancer surgery in 1810. Nine months after the event, Burney wrote an extremely intimate yet carefully observed description of her experience in a long letter to her sister. Because she survived the operation by thirty years, some commentators have suggested that her tumor may not have been malignant. See *The Journals and Letters of Fanny Burney (Madame d'Arblay)*, ed. Joyce Hemlow, with Curtis D. Cecil and Althea Douglas, vol. 6 (Oxford: Oxford University Press, 1975).

8   For a critical discussion of the radical mastectomy, see Joan Austoker, "'The Treatment of Choice': Breast Cancer Surgery, 1860–1985," *Society for the Social History of Medicine*, (December 1985): 100–107.

9   Medical literature extending from the Victorian to the early modern period attributes breast cancers not just to reproductive disorders but to any permissive behavior that undermined the idea of a woman's innate constitutional inferiority. Women's health manuals and medical textbooks pointed to a precipitating "derangement" such as "disturbed rest, exposure to cold, late hours, fatigue" that could force a tumor "to extend to a malignant state, and advance very rapidly" (E W Tuson, *The Structure and Functions of the Female Breast as They Relate to Its Health, Derangement and Disease* (London: John Churchill, 1846), 153–54. The use of birth control was another supposed culprit; see Caroll Smith-Rosenberg and Charles Rosenberg, "The Female Animal: Medical and Biological Views of Woman and Her Role

179

in Nineteenth-Century America," in *Women and Health in America: Historical Readings*, ed. Judith W. Leavitt (Madison: University of Wisconsin Press, 1984), 12–27.

10   The earliest observation connecting women who had never borne children with higher rates of breast cancer was made by an Italian in the seventeenth century. Another Italian physician, Rigoni-Stern, undertook a more thorough study of nuns that elaborated the same theme in the mid-nineteenth century. See Piero Mustacchi, "Ramazzini and Rigoni-Stern on Parity and Breast Cancer," *Archives of Internal Medicine* (October 1961): 639–42.

11   Joseph Schereschewsky, "The Course of Cancer Mortality in the Ten Original Registration States for the 21-Year Period, 1900–1920," *Public Health Bulletin* No. 155 (Washington, D.C.: Government Printing Office, 1925), 22, 67.

12   Quoted in Florence Converse, *Wellesley College: A Chronicle of the Years 1875–1938* (Wellesley, MA: Hathaway House Bookshop, 1939), 121.

13   Coman's book was first published in 1912; several later editions followed.

14   All references to Bates's diaries and letters are taken from documents in the Katharine Lee Bates Papers (henceforth KLBP).

15   The   college   honored   Coman   with   a   special

Memorial Supplement to the *Wellesley College News* in April 1915. It includes tributes from Jane Addams and Florence Kelley as well as a bibliography, reviews of her books, and two poems by Bates. Although Jane Addams is not mentioned in Bates's illness narrative, she was a friend to both Coman and Bates.

16   Shortly after his own retirement in 1905, Andrew Carnegie established the Carnegie Foundation for the Advancement of Teachers. Its purpose was to fund and administer a free, i.e., non-contributory pension plan for retiring academic faculty. Wellesley was one of the forty to fifty private institutions whose faculty members were eligible for this program.

17   Balch succeeded Coman as head of the Department of Economics. For a rich study of the Wellesley community of women, see Patricia Ann Palmieri, *In Adamless Eden: The Community of Women Faculty at Wellesley* (New Haven: Yale University Press, 1995).

18   Vida Scudder, *On Journey* (New York: E P Dutton, 1937), 298.

19   Dorothea Lawrance Mann, *Katharine Lee Bates: Poet and Professor*, repr. from *Boston Evening Transcript*, n.d. (Boston: Dorothea Lawrance Mann, 1931), 18.

20   Before the last quarter of the twentieth century, it was not customary for surgeons to share the details of their procedures with patients. See, for example, a letter written on 8 October 1918 by a mastectomy patient

describing the swelling of her arm, a post-operative development that apparently took her by surprise, although it was already a commonly known side effect of radical breast surgery. See Ellen Leopold, *A Darker Ribbon: Breast Cancer, Women and Their Doctors in the Twentieth Century* (Boston: Beacon, 1999), 99. Surgeons were particularly concerned not to frighten cancer patients away from what they considered lifesaving surgery. An equally important factor in preserving ignorance about the procedure was its relative rarity in 1911, when Coman was first treated. Not only was the incidence of disease rare, compared with today, surgery was even rarer. A significant proportion of diagnosed women went untreated. Some could not afford to pay for medical care; others were frightened of hospitals — they were still thought of as places where people went to die (and women did die from complications following mastectomies). Many waited too long after discovering a breast lump before seeking medical attention. By the time they saw a doctor, their tumors were deemed inoperable. In sum, the radical mastectomy was still too rare a procedure in 1911 for most women to have heard anything about it in advance of undergoing it.

21 Secrecy colored every aspect of the experience. A doctor writing in a woman's magazine twenty years after Coman's death used the cautionary tale of his own sister-in-law to plead for early detection. Having discovered a lump in her breast, she "felt that conditions of that sort prohibited consultations with anyone, even her husband. The lump had grown and had become hard and irregular in outline. Still she hid its existence

182

from every one" (Clarence C Little, "The Conquest of Cancer," *Good Housekeeping*, December 1936, 79). Not long after this, she died.

22 Bates shares her distress with her close friend Caroline Hazard in a letter written a week after Coman's second surgery."These are heavily troubled days, Dear Heart. . . . The future looks short and troubled . . . they had to make the operation as radical and extensive as possible. I can't bear to think of what they have done to her. She doesn't know it yet—poor dear!—and she's there congratulating herself that all is happily over" (8 June 1912, KLBP).

23 A week after Coman's first surgery, Bates noted in her diary that Katharine was "steadily gaining but now word comes that Mrs. Hamilton goes on Friday to that same table." The next day she noted that "Katharine is doing better and better but Mrs. Hamilton's eyes look as mine felt a week ago" (7 and 8 June 1911, KLBP). Mrs. Hamilton was the wife of Clarence C Hamilton of Wellesley's music department. He composed a musical setting to "America the Beautiful" of which Bates was fond (Burgess, *Dream and Deed*, 105).

24 Active in her local church, St. Andrew's in Wellesley, Coman conducted informal Bible classes with interested students but eschewed theological dogmatism: "Faith was indeed a word more native to her than creed." Vida Scudder, "'Religious Life.' In Memoriam: Katharine Coman," *Wellesley College News*, April 1915, 21–23.

25   The line quoted is from Psalm 57, which reads, in part, "Be merciful unto me, O God, be merciful unto me: for my soul trusteth in thee: yea, in the shadow of thy wings will I make my refuge, until these calamities be overpast. . . . My soul is among lions: and I lie even among them that are set on fire, even the sons of men, whose teeth are spears and arrows, and their tongue a sharp sword" (1, 4). See Katharine Lee Bates, *Yellow Clover: A Book of Remembrance.* (New York: E P Dutton, 1922), 76.

26   The poem first appeared with this title in November 1915 in the *Countryside Magazine and Suburban Life* (263); it reappeared as "Pointed Firs" in *Yellow Clover*, 51.

27   Marian W Flexner, "Cancer—I've Had It," *Ladies' Home Journal,* May 1947, 57, 150. For more on the earliest published accounts of breast cancer see Leopold, *A Darker Ribbon,* chap. 7.

28   See Katharine Lee Bates, *The Retinue and Other Poems* (New York: E P Dutton, 1918).

2   "FOR KATHARINE COMAN'S FAMILY AND INNERMOST CIRCLE OF FRIENDS"
29   Cornelia Warren worked with Coman on the Boston settlement house. She was a civic–minded philanthropist who bequeathed 75 acres of her estate in Waltham, Massachusetts, to the Girl Scouts in 1923.

30   Katharine Raymond was another member of the

University of Michigan contingent at Wellesley that included Coman herself and Eliza Mosher, another physician. She taught Hygiene at the college and served as its resident physician from 1907 to 1925. At her death, Bates wrote a tribute for the *Boston Evening Transcript* of 6 April 1925.

31   Coman gave the name "Bohemia" to her own sunny room at the top of the Scarab. After Coman's death Bates moved her study into it and, fourteen years later, died in it.

32   Coman, while convalescing, worked hard to raise money to get her kindergarten project under way. Finally, a friend, Helen Craig, agreed to lend the necessary support. "If you will supply the building and equipment for the kindergarten," Craig wrote, "I will supply the teacher." With the help of the Wellesley Village Improvement Society, a provisional location was secured and equipped and a teacher hired. A year later Wellesley College Trustees agreed to build a permanent home for the project on the college campus. The building would serve as an innovative practice school tied in to the college's education curriculum. The nursery still operates today in the same building, now known as the Child Study Center. "The Anne L. Page Memorial: Department of Education Wellesley College," Wellesley, Massachusetts, 1913–1930.

33   See note 16.

34   Katharine Coman, *Memories of Martha Seymour*

Coman (Boston: Fort Hill Press, 1913).

35   This work had been suggested to her by Jane Addams, who had also introduced her, many years earlier, to settlement work.

36   Olga Halsey, a 1912 Wellesley graduate, worked for the federal government for almost three decades as a labor researcher and administrator. She helped to draft the Social Security bill enacted by Congress in 1935. In a Wellesley alumnae publication, she wrote of her career, "I owe my pioneer start in social insurance legislation to the late Prof. Coman who, shortly after my graduation, asked me to accompany her to Europe as an assistant in the study of European social insurance which she was making at the suggestion of Jane Addams." Wellesley College Archives.

37   William Sampson Handley (1872–1962) was a prominent cancer surgeon in London who carried out research into various cancers, including breast cancer, at the Middlesex Hospital. He provided conceptual underpinning for the use of the radical mastectomy. Though his theory of the disease turned out to be mistaken, the procedure both he and Halsted routinely performed remained the almost universal treatment for breast cancer for three-quarters of a century.

38   Psalms 57:4.

39   Like Katharine Raymond, Eliza Mosher obtained her medical degree at the University of Michigan. Since

she was a physician and had herself undergone cancer surgery more than twenty years earlier, she might have been a source of special hopefulness to Coman.

40   This Katharine is the daughter of her sister Susan Coman Coburn.

41   Ellis B. Dean was the rector at St. Andrew's Church, Wellesley, Massachusetts.

42   Marion Pelton Guild was an alumna trustee of Wellesley College. After Bates died, she selected poems and edited what would be the last volume of Bates's published poetry, *Selected Poems* (Boston: Houghton Mifflin, 1930).

43   This may have been *The Blue Bird*, a silent film made in 1910 based on a novel by Maeterlinck.

44   *The Raft*, by the English-born Coningsby Dawson (1883–1959) had just been published (1914) when Bates read it to Coman. Dawson wrote several books on the First World War in which he served as an Infantryman.

45   Christina G. Rossetti, "God Is Our Hope and Strength."

46   John Greenleaf Whittier, "The Eternal Goodness." Bates has inverted the order of these two stanzas.

47   Deuteronomy 33:27

4 IRMA NATANSON AND THE LEGAL LAND-MARK *NATANSON V. KLINE*

48 There is a fuller version of Natanson's ordeal in my book *Under the Radar: Cancer and the Cold War* (New Brunswick, NJ: Rutgers University Press, 2009).

49 The details of the case, *Natanson v. Kline* (350P 2d 1093, Kan. 1960), and all legal quotations are drawn from the trial proceedings and from Jay Katz, *The Silent World of Doctor and Patient* (Baltimore: Johns Hopkins University Press, 2002), chap. 3.

50 Newer lawsuits against radiologists are often related to mammograms. The suits are a result of overselling the promise of screening mammography, especially to younger women for whom screening fails to pick up 15 to 20 percent of breast cancers.

5 BARBIE MEETS BREAST CANCER

51 Ruth Handler with Jacqueline Shannon, *Dream Doll: The Ruth Handler Story* (Stamford, CT: Longmeadow Press, 1994), 212–13.

52 When Handler retired in 1991, she sold the company to Spenco Medical Corporation. Today it survives as Nearly Me Technologies. It now offers prostheses made of whipped silicone, which significantly reduces the weight of earlier models.

53 Healey's argument can be found in an article that is available, after free registration, at Medscape, http://www.medscape.com/viewarticle/460148_1.

6 BODY LANGUAGE

54 Bill Keller, "Heroic Measures," *New York Times* 12 January 2014. Emma Keller's blog, posted on 8 January was taken down from the *Guardian* website on 13 January after Bonchek Adams alerted the editor to several inaccuracies in the Keller column.

55 Two of the diarists discussed in this article died of their disease—Rosalind MacPhee at age 50, in 1996, the year her book was published, and Christina Middlebrook, at age 67, in 2009, almost twenty years after her diagnosis.

7 THE LAST WORD

56 Virginia Woolf, *A Room of One's Own* (New York: Harcourt Brace, 1989), 50. Woolf's sister, the painter Vanessa Bell, died of breast cancer in 1961.

57 Because this story has been traced primarily through the pages of the *New York Times*, it offers a largely white and middle-class portrait of women with cancer.

58 Cited in Leslie J Reagan, "Engendering the Dread Disease: Women, Men and Cancer," *American Journal of Public Health* 87/11 (1997): 1779–87.

59 *New York Times*, 23 September 1974.

60   Among the many achievements of Rose Kushner (1929–1990) was her ultimately successful assault on the then almost universal "one–step" surgical protocol for women with suspected breast cancer. This was the practice of carrying out a biopsy on a woman who lay unconscious on the operating table and then, if the results were positive for cancer, proceeding directly to a radical mastectomy, without conferring with the patient at all. Kushner argued that *"separating biopsy from mastectomy gives women a voice in controlling their own destinies"* (italics hers). Rose Kushner, *Breast Cancer: A Personal History and an Investigative Report* (New York: Harcourt Brace Jovanovich, 1975), 346.

61   Letter from Rachel Carson to Marjorie Spock and Polly Richards, 12 April 1960, Rachel Carson Papers, Beinicke Library, Yale University.

62   *New York Times*, 20 May 2013.

8   SHOPPING FOR THE CURE
63   For more about the NBCCEDP see http://www.cdc.gov/cancer/nbccedp/data/summaries/, accessed 12 February 2014.

10   THE BREAST CANCER DONOR'S DILEMMA
64   In 1969, there were 2,250 United Funds in the United States, with 33 million contributors. Jerry M. Flint, "Charity Drives Criticized About Middle-Class Goals; Institutional Charity Is Meeting Rising Unrest in Nation Over Middle-Class Goals," *New York Times*, 3 November 1969.

65   In 1949, the three independent campaigns of the Red Cross, March of Dimes, and Christmas Seals raised a combined total of $113 million, compared with a total of $188 million raised by over 1,000 community chests. F Emerson Andrews, *Philanthropic Giving* (New York: Russell Sage Foundation, 1950), 153.

66   Polly Brody Temkin, "The Housewives' Revolt," *The Progressive*, February 1966, 28–31.

67   See "Charities Working to Prevent and Cure Breast Cancer," on the Charity Navigator website.

68   See Barbara Brenner's blog, "Has NBCC Lost Its Way?" on her website "Healthy Barbs."

69   For the U.S. Preventive Services Task Force Recommendations, see http://www.uspreventiveservicestaskforce.org/uspstf/ uspsbrca.htm.   For Breast Cancer Action's screening recommendations, see http://bcaction.org/wp-content/ uploads/2011/01/BCA-Screening-Policy-Final-2010.pdf

Made in the USA
Lexington, KY
17 April 2014